Oxford Studies of Composers (20)

CARISSIMI

GRAHAM DIXON

Oxford New York
OXFORD UNIVERSITY PRESS
1986

Oxford University Press, Walton Street, Oxford OX2 6DP
Oxford New York Toronto
Delhi Bombay Calcutta Madras Karachi
Kuala Lumpur Singapore Hong Kong Tokyo
Nairobi Dar es Salaam Cape Town
Melbourne Auckland
and associated companies in
Beirut Berlin Ibadan Nicosia

OXFORD is a trade mark of Oxford University Press

© Graham Dixon 1986

British Library Cataloguing in Publication Data

Dixon, Graham
Carissimi.—(Oxford studies of composers)
1. Carissimi, Giacomo
I. Title
780'.92'4 ML410.C3/
ISBN 0–19–315249–5
ISBN 0–19–315243–6 Pbk

Library of Congress Cataloging in Publication Data

Dixon, Graham.
Carissimi.
((Oxford studies of composers; 1)
Bibliography; p.
Includes index.
1. Carissimi, Giacomo, 1605–1674.
2. Composers—Itality—Biography
I. Title.
II. Series.
ML410.C3268D6 1985 783'.092'4 [B] 85–7202
ISBN 0–19–315249–5
ISBN 0–19–315243–6 (pbk.)

Set by Hope Services, Abingdon
Printed and bound in Great Britain
by Biddles Ltd.,
Guildford and King's Lynn

CONTENTS

For Helen

PREFATORY NOTE

A<small>NY</small> discussion of a composer poses considerable problems when he has as many doubtful works attributed to his name as reliably attested ones. No short monograph can provide sufficient space to deal with the problems of attribution, and I have therefore confined my discussion of Carissimi's music to those works widely accepted as authentic. I therefore gratefully acknowledge my debt to the manuscript studies of Dr Andrew Jones and the late Dr Gloria Rose, which have provided a sound foundation for my study. The term 'soprano' is used throughout to indicate the vocal range, not the type of voice which would generally have performed the music. I have used the spelling 'Iacomo' for Carissimi's Christian name, since even in his own day Carissimi declined to spell it in the conventional manner. I would like to thank Michael Talbot and Basil Smallman for their advice and encouragement. I am also particularly indebted to the staffs at the Music Library of the University of Birmingham and the Civico Museo Bibliografico Musicale of Bologna for their invaluable assistance.

I
INTRODUCTION: *Roma triumphans*

SIX years after Urban VIII was elected to the See of Peter, Iacomo Carissimi (1605–74), one of the greatest musical figures to emerge in Baroque Rome, became maestro at the German College. To many his appointment in December 1629 must have seemed a peculiar decision; certainly Bernardino Castorio, Rector of the College, was taking a considerable risk in giving the post to a young musician who had neither proved himself in Rome nor had any published music to his credit. Yet Carissimi was equal to his new task and took advantage of the singularly favourable environment in which he found himself.

Rome in the 1620s was a good place for the musician or artist: the seemingly arrested growth of Protestantism and the success of foreign missions meant that Counter-Reformation austerity was taken over by a new wave of optimism. Urban VIII, a notable patron of music, was responsible for the initiation of the Roman opera, and his pontificate carried with it a second period of Renaissance in which creative activity flourished. The triumphal spirit found artistic and musical expression, not least in the embellishment of the newly completed basilica of St Peter's and in new churches built to honour the saints of the period of Reform. In fact Carissimi's appointment could not have come at a more opportune moment, for, having cast aside the stern regime of the late sixteenth century, the church had not yet fallen into the easygoing quietism which characterized the second half of the seventeenth.

Carissimi may well have felt daunted by the proud tradition of music at the German College:[1] Victoria and Ruggiero Giovannelli had been among the first maestri, and in the early years of the century the College had employed Agostino Agazzari and Antonio Cifra, two important pioneers of the small-scale motet—a prominent genre in Italian church music throughout the Baroque. Lorenzo Ratti, Carissimi's immediate predecessor, had left a similar position at the wealthy French church in Rome, San Luigi dei

Francesi, in favour of one at the College in 1623. As early as 1608 the services there were 'frequented by cardinals, ambassadors of princes, prelates, etc.', who were attracted by the music;[2] and in Panciroli's guide to Rome of 1600 the church was singled out for the same reason.[3] Many similar accounts by travellers and in guide-books survive from Carissimi's time as maestro, an appointment he held until his death. Carissimi's previous experience had been rather limited: born at Marino near Rome in 1605, he was active as a singer and organist at Tivoli for about four years (1623–7),[4] and then at the cathedral in Assisi until 1629.

The German College, with its professional *cappella* of around ten singers, augmented by student voices, enjoyed a richness of musical activity not shared by the majority of religious institutions. Singers and instrumentalists from outside were often called in at festivals, and it seems that the instrumental tradition was stronger there than in almost all other churches. Agazzari and Annibale Orgas, two maestri of the College, were among the handful of Roman composers to specify the use of instruments in their works. Music at the College was greatly encouraged by two events which occurred in 1573: the endowment of the College on its re-establishment by Gregory XIII, and the appointment as Rector of Michael Lauretano, a man convinced of the value of thorough liturgical observance. The German College came to serve as a model of liturgical practice for Jesuit institutions throughout Europe. It was an exceptional case, since within it there was both an enthusiasm for liturgy and the financial resources necessary to employ competent musicians for liturgical adornment.

Most churches were not so fortunate, and had to suffer the efforts of inadequately trained *cappellani* singing plainsong, except once or twice a year on festivals, when a choir of outsiders was hired. Despite the historical importance of music performed in the churches and oratories of the flourishing Roman brotherhoods, most of the musical forces consisted of free-lance musicians hired for particular occasions. The maestro of a church would often take the members of his *cappella*, or even a more *ad hoc* group, to sing at another church on a patronal festival. This, then, was the context for Carissimi's Latin oratorios, written for the Arciconfraternita del Santissimo Crocifisso, which seems to have had no resident musicians. The main concern of this body, as with many confraternities, was Lenten observance, and here in particular the Fridays of Lent. It is consistent with our knowledge of musicians' activities to imagine that when Carissimi composed music for this *oratorio*, he also organized a group of musicians and directed the performance. It is not inconceivable that some of his Lenten pieces on Latin texts were written for the German College itself: the Rector referred to an ancient tradition of Lenten music there in a letter of 1610,[5] and expressed anxiety that the Santissimo Crocifisso was threatening to disrupt this by hiring the putti of the College for their devotions on the same evenings.

While Carissimi spent most of his time in the service of the German College, and visited other religious institutions on an occasional basis, he also devoted some time to secular music. He had composed secular cantatas at least as early as 1640, but with the arrival of Christine of Sweden in Rome in 1655, and his appointment at her court in the following year, this aspect of his activity was presumably encouraged. The central position that he holds in the genres of the oratorio, motet, and cantata provides a good starting point for an examination of music in Baroque Rome. At the same time it is essential to realize that he was no isolated figure, but simply one of the large number of musicians (many of whom are all but forgotten) who served the churches, seminaries, confraternities, and courts of the city.

Over three hundred years have passed since the death of Carissimi, and until now there has been no monograph devoted to his music as a whole. This is due, at least in part, to difficulties with the surviving musical sources and problems of attribution. Perhaps on account of his early success, Carissimi had little of his music printed; he had no need to flatter patrons to secure preferment as did many of his contemporaries. Only two volumes of his music were published in his lifetime, besides a number of pieces in anthologies. The policy of keeping his music in manuscript in the German College, in accordance with a papal brief, was intended as a measure to preserve it, but unfortunately had the opposite effect. Access to the archives was restricted and copying prevented, so that when the documents disappeared in the eighteenth century the music was less well disseminated than it otherwise would have been. Despite numerous problems of attribution caused by the disparate nature of the sources, it is possible to establish a central corpus of works about which there is little doubt. This volume is concerned with a representative cross-section of these pieces.

II
MUSICAL STYLE

DISCUSSIONS of Carissimi's stylistic procedures have generally centred on *Figurenlehre*, the extent to which musical motifs reflect the conventions of the highly formalized art of Rhetoric.[1] This concern with the structure of the musical phrase has diverted attention from more central issues of texture, sonority, and overall planning. One has to look no further than the works of Palestrina (d. 1594) to see how far Carissimi's compositional idiom differs from that of the sixteenth century. There is none of the conservatism often mistakenly associated with Rome in this period: crisp, energetic rhythms have replaced fluid metres; monody and a vertical view of texture have taken the place of smooth counterpoint. Moreover there is no laboured reworking of the Palestrina style that some textbooks would lead us to expect in seventeenth-century Rome; the codification of Fux had not yet encroached upon composers' spontaneity. While there are dangers in talking of style in abstract terms, unrelated to musical genres and their context, it may be useful to outline some of the stylistic changes that occurred between the time of Palestrina and of Carissimi, a subject which has received scant attention from music historians.

Carissimi belongs to a succession of Roman church musicians who, in matters of musical style and taste, were essentially pragmatists. They were not given to the elaborate theorizing of the Florentines or caught up in the polemics of the *seconda prattica* waged by Artusi and Monteverdi. The Romans' chief concern, and indeed duty, was to provide and perform music in the light of the prevailing performance conditions; as such, it was of little consequence which canon of theoretical presuppositions was followed. At the beginning of the seventeenth century, churches were struggling to maintain a decent musical tradition: the demands of intricate counterpoint were too much for many choirs, and a number were forced to sing polyphony omitting some of the parts—a far from satisfactory state of affairs. It was as an attempt to relieve the strain on choirs that the few-voiced motet was introduced in Rome in the 1590s. None of the lofty Florentine concerns about the revival of Greek music was inherent in the adoption of this new idiom. It owed its popularity to the fact that the organ, or other continuo instrument, could fuse the musical texture, thus obviating the need for a cohesive, flowing polyphonic style with a larger number of voices. The new scaled-down style was an immediate success. Lodovico Viadana, the originator of the idiom, remarked on the demand for his own works in a preface in 1602;[2] he was soon followed into print by two of Carissimi's predecessors at the German College, Agazzari and Cifra. In 1606 Agazzari became the first composer to publish small-scale motets in Rome, and he issued a treatise on the value of the *basso continuo* in the following year. Cifra published four books of motets for two to four voices in 1609; within ten years these were followed by five more collections.

Composers working at the German College did not have to contend with the lack of resources which fired initial enthusiasm for the medium. However, from the outset, Agazzari had regarded the idiom as a potent way of expressing the text; it seems that the duet and trio media were soon accepted on account of their intrinsic merits and not simply as a stand-by when polyphony could not be managed. The flexibility of the style and the possibilities which it offered the individual voice compounded its attractiveness: vocal parts became less like strands drawn from polyphonic motets and acquired a new, altogether different sense of line and balance. In this connection it is worth comparing the incipit of Giovanni Francesco Anerio's 1609 solo motet *Cantabo Domino* with a reworking of it he published in 1620 (Ex. 1).[3] The search for a flexible idiom was extended in the 1630s when the trio came increasingly to the fore, replacing the duet as the preferred medium. Three voices offered a greater variety of vocal groupings. In keeping with this trend well over a third of Carissimi's motets are scored for three voices, while fewer than a third use two parts; all need continuo.

With the acceptance of the small-scale idiom as more than an enforced compromise between polyphony and chant, it became natural to incorporate reduced sections into pieces for a greater number of voices. Such music was performed in institutions with a developed choral tradition, and the variety was part of its appeal. A diagram of the vocal entries in Agazzari's *Domine Dominus noster* (1613)[4] gives an idea of this procedure. This juxtaposition of

Ex. 1 (Continuo omitted)

1609

Can - ta - - - - - bo Do - mi - no

1620

Can - ta - - - - - bo Do - mi - no

Voice parts in Agazzari, *Domine Dominus noster*

S ——————   ——————————   ———————   ————————
S ——————   ————   ————   ——————————
A — ——   ————————   —   ———————
T ————————   ————   ————   ————————
T — ——   ————   —   ——————
B — ——   ————————   ——————————   ——————————

textures (known, at least in Rome, as the *concertato* style) was of great consequence for the motet style of Carissimi, but even more so for his oratorios, where the dramatic sequence could be reflected by changes in scoring. Initially changes of texture took place within a single section, but another technique, that of dividing the motet into a number of self-contained movements, became increasingly common. Virgilio Mazzocchi's *Filiae Jerusalem* (1645)[5] is an example of this type of organization:

Filiae Jerusalem	A
Quo abiit	TT
Formosum vidimus	ATTB
Adjuro vos	B
Vox dilecti mei	A
Surge propera	ATTB

By the time Carissimi arrived in Rome these devices, that is, the use of reduced textures and the *concertato* idiom, were well established. No composer could afford to ignore them, and they were generally appreciated, except in the Sistine Chapel, where an archaic style persisted.

While the continuo became commonplace, there are only a few

pieces by Carissimi which include other instrumental parts. Romans seem to have been considerably more reluctant than their North Italian contemporaries to introduce obbligato lines, though church archives record that a variety of instruments performed in festal music. The violin was accepted in church and chamber in the 1620s, and the earliest printed violin part in a secular piece appears in Paolo Quagliati's *Sfera armoniosa* of 1623. Published Roman church music with instrumental parts from before 1645 amounts to a set of psalms by Paolo Tarditi and four motets. A number of motets by Carissimi (some dating from before 1636) have violin parts, as do some of the oratorios, but only a few cantatas with violins survive. Motet anthologies from the late 1640s contain occasional pieces with two violins, but, if his surviving works are any indication, Carissimi does not seem to have had much interest in obbligato parts. Francis Mortoft, an English traveller to Rome in 1659, witnessed the use of 'Lute, Violl, and two Violins' at the Santissimo Crocifisso;[6] this concurs with the higher proportion of instrumental parts in Carissimi's oratorios than in the other genres he employed.

Monody was an essential part of the narrative and dialogue of the oratorios. While following the Roman tendency to avoid the solo motet, Carissimi used the solo voice with continuo to good effect in the oratorios and the cantatas; most of the latter are for solo performance. Here, and in the dramatic oratorios, there was no need to maintain the objectivity necessary for the liturgy: in fact the oratorios contain many deeply emotional moments (the lament of Jephthah's daughter, the prayer of Jonah) which would have been out of place in motets for liturgical use.[7] In the cantatas Carissimi adopts an even more flexible monodic style; the personalized expression of the solo singer is entirely apt since the texts generally consist of the outpourings of forlorn lovers.

The monodic style was well accepted in Rome by Carissimi's time: on his return from Florence Emilio de' Cavalieri had his famous *Rappresentatione di anima et di corpo* performed there in 1600. This was followed by the publication of Ottavio Durante's book of spiritual *arie* (1608) and Kapsberger's sacred and secular works. Landi consolidated the Roman monodic style in his *Arie* (1620) and his operas; and it was he, together with Luigi Rossi, who laid one of the foundations for Carissimi's secular monodic style. In church music, however, a genuine monodic freedom was slower to emerge: composers either remained hidebound by the sense of contrapuntal line, as did G. F. Anerio in his 1618 motets, or wrote insignificant roulades, like Ratti. The latter's one solo motet, *Jesu dulcedo* (1628) (Ex. 2), demonstrates the excesses of this

Ex. 2 (Continuo omitted)

O dul - ce re - - - - - - - - - [frigerium]

style.[8] Carissimi managed to steer a course between these extremes, and, while injecting considerable movement and interest into the lines, he managed to check any tendency towards frivolous embellishment. His monody moves judiciously between a plain narrative style, a rather more affective idiom for moments of textual tension, and a song-like manner usually associated with triple metre. At the opening of *Baltazar* the narrative style continues until the words mention music; at this point there is a change of metre and tonality (Ex. 3). The affective idiom, of which

Ex. 3

Historicus

su-per-bo lu- xu et lau-tis-si-mis e -pu-lis magni-fi-ce in-struc-tum

bc

dul - ci - - so-nis in - - te-rim

examples abound, employs a range of devices among which can be listed ascending and descending chromatic lines; lines which incorporate unusual melodic intervals or which leap on to a dissonance; and repetition of a phrase one tone higher.

As already noted, the usual way to examine Carissimi's music has been through the recognition of figures within the musical phrase. The justification of this method lies in the way it elucidates the structures used by the composer in his musical rhetoric. In Carissimi's music we can no longer perceive the Monteverdian ideal of music as simply serving the words; rather, the rhetorical dimension inherent in the text is underscored and impressed upon the listener by the use of corresponding musical features. One extended example (Ex. 4) can serve to show this. The form of this

Ex. 4

Ex. 4 (*cont.*):

text, the Historicus's introduction to *Judicium Salomonis*, dictates, to some extent at least, the formal scheme of the music:

A solis ortu et ab occasu
venite populi, properate gentes
et sapientiam magni regis et Judicium Salomonis audite
et sapientiam magni regis et Judicium Salomonis audite.
Ante regem duae steterunt infelices genetrices   5
hululantes, hululantes et clamantes sic dixerunt,
ante regem duae steterunt,
ante regem duae steterunt infelices genetrices
hululantes, hululantes, hululantes et clamantes sic dixerunt,
hululantes, hululantes et clamantes sic dixerunt . . .   10

The text is not biblical, but a call to attend to the story which ensues. Lines 2, 3, and 4 contain *parallelisma*, emphasized in lines 3 and 4 by the repetition of the conjunction 'et'. The music reflects these features: the same motif is used twice in line 2, the second time raised by a fourth; the setting of line 4 uses the same phrase as line 3 but again modified by transposition (*epizeuxis*). The most striking rhetorical feature in the second half (lines 5–10) is the repetition of the word 'hululantes'; this reaches a climax in line 9 where it appears three times. Each occurrence is presented at a higher musical pitch, and at the same time the bass has the musical device of *pathopoeia*, rising and descending chromatic lines. The setting of line 7 anticipates that of the following line, by using the same phrase a fourth lower. One musical feature, *hypotyposis* or word-painting, has no rhetorical equivalent; this appears at the beginning of the passage, where the rapid rise and fall in the vocal line depicts the rising and setting of the sun, metaphorically used here to signify East and West.

The device of *epizeuxis* or transposition has some bearing upon an understanding of tonality in Carissimi's works. Clearly the regular transpositions, usually by the intervals of a fourth and a fifth, serve to reinforce a sense of tonal feeling. Yet, even before Carissimi's time, a growing assimilation of tonal procedures in music, with a degree of major-minor polarity, can be detected. Composers' reliance on chant as a basis for composition was steadily diminishing throughout the early *Seicento*, even in those genres where it was considered most appropriate, such as psalm-settings. In the first two decades of the century it would have been surprising to find a psalm which did not contain at least a passing reference to an appropriate psalm-tone; but by the 1640s status of chant as a compositional basis was so weakened that Filippo da Cavi, for example, could write a *Dixit Dominus* in what (even now) would pass for F minor.[9] Carissimi's lengthy cantata *Ahi non torna* (SS) also uses an F minor tonality, emphasizing the unusual nature of the harmony with its false relations and diminished chords. Often it is within the more common tonalities that Carissimi introduces his least conventional writing: in the G minor *Inventane più* (S), a solo cantata, he introduces a D^b for the phrase 'respirar sua crudeltà' (breathe his cruelty), which is then transposed by a fourth. In the same cantata the word 'pene' (torments) is not only set to a falling sixth, but also elicits an F-F$^{\sharp}$ chromatic alteration. His church music is generally more reserved in this respect, though when imaginative harmonic devices occur they are all the more striking: an example of this is the phrase 'mori dignatus est' in *Surrexit Pastor bonus* (SSS) with its minor tonality.

Another feature of the Baroque style much associated with the music of Carissimi is the tendency towards a vertical, harmonic view of texture, as opposed to a horizontal, polyphonic one. This is shown clearly in the large-scale choruses of the oratorios which feature decisive homorhythmic declamation, an aspect of his style assimilated by his pupil Marc-Antoine Charpentier in his *histoires sacrées*.[10] The introduction of the continuo went hand in hand with this development, and in Rome the use of this vertical style was prompted by two factors: the flourishing polychoral idiom, and the growing interest in setting Vespers psalms. The concept of a choir as a block of sound in multiple-choir music initiated a species of confident four-part writing. Each choir responded to the others with a pithy series of chords; the main interest was the spatial element, not the musical content of each voice part. Vespers psalms were problematic to the composer on account of the length of their texts. The main concern was to set the text at a reasonable pace; as a result the reflection of any subtleties of textual meaning took second place. The expressive possibilities of an idiom employing repeated notes (*stile concitato*) were realized even before Monteverdi's *Combattimento di Tancredi e Clorinda* (1624); as early as 1616 the Roman Abundio Antonelli chose to represent the stoning of Stephen in this way.[11] Ottavio Catalani, a former maestro at the German College, incorporated the same principle into a larger canvas in his paean on the slaying of the Philistines, *Percussit Saul mille*—an anticipation of the battles of *Jephte* (Ex. 5).[12]

Ex. 5

As with Monteverdi, Carissimi's motivation in employing a new muscial style was its capacity for supporting the general concepts enshrined in the text. Carissimi's choruses certainly show that the two composers would have agreed about the effect of the *stile concitato*, a theoretical exposition of which is found in the preface to Monteverdi's *Madrigali guerrieri et amorosi* (1638).

A historical approach to the analysis of mid-Baroque music, and particularly that of Carissimi, relies on this concept of affects (or affections). The first theorist to discuss the works of Carissimi in print, the Jesuit scholar Athanasius Kircher, noted that Carissimi 'surpasses all others in moving the minds of the listeners to whatever affection he wishes'.[13] He cites in illustration of this the famous final chorus of *Jephte* and the cantata *A piè d'un verde alloro.* In the former work the mood suddenly shifts from victory to grief as Jephthah's daughter appears; in the latter the contrast of joy and sadness is again represented by a change from major to minor. In *Jephte* this shift also appears in the recitative, where a minor third is introduced in the sixth bar (Ex. 6). The fact that this example is

Ex. 6

preceded by a joyous six-part chorus in G major serves to highlight the abrupt change. Kircher's view was that music was capable of portraying eight affects: love, lamentation, joy, indignation, pity, fear, boldness, and wonder.[14] Perhaps this statement of Carissimi's distinguished Jesuit contemporary, emphasizing the discrete types of musical representation, can lead us to an understanding of Carissimi's music.

III
LITURGICAL MUSIC

As maestro at the German College Carissimi would have devoted a good deal of effort to providing music for the *cappella* of this, one of the foremost centres of liturgical music in Rome. Yet most of his output survives only in manuscript, with the attendant problems of attribution. As indicated above, the scarcity of printed sources for Carissimi's music is perhaps due to his appointment to the German College so early in his career. Having reached this respected position, he had no need to ingratiate himself with potential patrons through flattering dedications, and it was apparently a matter of little consequence to him whether or not his music was heard more widely. He seems in some respects to have been a man of little ambition, judging by the attractive offers he declined.[1] Despite the lively artistic atmosphere in Rome, his appointment to the College happened at the beginning of a barren period for the publication of church music. The single-composer collections of the early part of the century had almost vanished, and it was not until the 1640s that they were replaced by a succession of motet anthologies. Carissimi contributed to a number of these, but was quite advanced in years before any publications were devoted solely to his music.

Like most of his contemporaries he was more concerned with the composition of motets than masses. Study of his masses has been particularly bedevilled by the lack of attributions in manuscript sources. Some years ago it was claimed with confidence that Carissimi had written twelve masses,[2] whereas *New Grove* asserts that only three are indisputably his. Recently serious doubts have been cast on the authorship of one of the remaining three, the *Missa a quinque et a novem*. In fact the *Missa 'Sciolto havean dall'alte sponde'*, though an unusually late example of parody technique, is the only mass whose authenticity lies beyond any reasonable doubt. Based on the widely circulated cantata of the same name, it is designated 'a 5 con ripieni, e sinfonia'. The scoring is SSATB, SATB with the addition of two violins: musical material is concentrated in the first, five-part choir, which has responsibility for all the solo passages, while the second choir reinforces the texture with occasional doubling. Typical of Carissimi's handling of the musical forces is the setting of 'miserere nobis' in the Gloria, where, following an imitative build-up in the first choir, the second enters in homophony together with the violins—this happens at each supplication (Ex. 7). The mass is based on the opening and

Ex. 7

concluding trios of the cantata, and the recitative style present elsewhere in the model is not adapted for the mass. The triple metre of these trios is frequently translated into common time, and their rigid homophonic idiom is clothed with some contrapuntal movement. The first Kyrie, based on the opening of the cantata, demonstrates these features, and there also appears Carissimi's characteristic transposition of material on the repeat of the opening phrase, a device not employed in the original cantata. This full section—with frequent trio interpolations—is based on the 'e cader' and 'per tributo' motifs of the cantata, while the five-part Christe (separated from the Kyries by instrumental sinfonias) develops the 'Amanti che dite' motif of the cantata's final trio. In a way similar to Carissimi's mass, Silvestro Durante's optional addition of a four-part choir to his five-part *Missa 'Corre la nave mia'* shows in its extensive vocal doublings a typical approach to the deployment of voices in the Roman 'colossal Baroque';[3] it also sheds light on the emergence of the *concerto grosso* in the same city.

The authorship of another mass for similar forces, long thought to be by Carissimi, has recently been challenged.[4] True, the violin parts of the *Missa a quinque et a novem*, published under Carissimi's name in 1665/6, contain some awkward moments, yet the scoring is Roman enough, and it is hard to imagine a false attribution appearing in the composer's lifetime. There are, however, problems with this work: if one accepts that it was originally for three voices, and that the two violins and optional four-part choir are spurious later additions, then the 'original' three lines (published as *Missa a 3*) have in places insufficient movement to sustain the texture. However, the string writing is rather makeshift, and the use of extended bass *ostinati* is uncharacteristic of Carissimi's style.[5] The arguments for and against his authorship are strong, and so extreme caution is needed before accepting Witzenmann's outright dismissal of the work. Perhaps this mass has come down to us through the chance dissemination of a hastily produced mass for some feast-day at the German College.

Despite the frequent singing of Vespers at the College, Carissimi left little music for this office. Only Vespers psalms remain (wrongly categorized as motets in *New Grove*): two settings of *Dixit Dominus* (SSATB and SATB, SATB) and one *Confitebor tibi* (SSB). These are clearly intended for liturgical use since they set the entire text with 'Gloria Patri'. While the *Confitebor tibi* is quite motet-like in style, *Dixit Dominus* (SSATB), the first psalm of festal Vespers, is a five-part setting in the sectionalized *concertato* idiom. It has some features in common with the few other settings of the same text to survive from this period. In common with double-choir versions by Foggia and Stefano Fabri,[6] each verse is a separate movement:

| Dixit Dominus | SSATB |
| Donec ponam | B |

Virgam virtutis	SS
Tecum principium	A (two versions with varying degrees of embellishment)
Juravit Dominus	SSATB (punctuated with SS solos)
Dominus a dextris	S₂
Judicabit in nationibus	S₁
De torrente	SSATB
Gloria Patri	T
Sicut erat	SSATB

Moreover, the sixth psalm tone emerges prominently at the opening to compensate for the absence of the intonation (Ex. 8).

Ex. 8

Carissimi rarely uses plainsong; apart from this example, it only appears in the three-part *Confitebor tibi* and *Salve regina* (SSB), and then it is no more than an initial motif.

In the setting of the first six verses of *In te Domine speravi* (Psalm 30) chant is replaced by a recurring note pattern. Though it is set with 'Gloria Patri', there is no suitable liturgical context for its performance since it does not belong to any of the commonly sung offices. The scoring is ATB, two violins and continuo, with lively exchanges between the voices and instruments. The two groups generally alternate, the continuo providing support for both, though at the climax of the work, 'accelera ut eruas me' (make haste to rescue me) they combine in spirited counterpoint, using the semiquaver motif which underlines the word 'accelera'. Some of the vocal writing takes on an instrumental character through the free transfer of material; the phrase with rests in the final Amen is an exact repeat of the preceding instrumental line (Ex. 9).

Ex. 9 (Continuo omitted)

It was on the motet, rather than other genres of church music, that Carissimi lavished most attention; such a bias is notable, too, in the output of his contemporaries, and it is not surprising that Carissimi wrote almost one hundred authenticated motets as opposed to his scant contribution to other genres of sacred music. Like his earliest mentor, Alessandro Capece, he specialized in small-scale music and regarded the continuo as indispensible; fewer than ten motets survive for more than four voices, and this despite the fact that more than six hundred *scudi* a year were spent at the German College maintaining a 'roomful of castrati', two organs, and three choirs.[7] The explanation for this paucity of surviving sources is that large-scale works were treated as occasional music and no trouble was taken to preserve the scores. We can assume, however, that Carissimi wrote willingly for small forces on account of the possibilities that these offered for characterization and the scope which they allowed individual voices. Of his extant motets thirty-one are for two voices, thirty-seven for three, seven for four, and fourteen are solo pieces. *Christus factus est* is one of two double-choir motets to survive: after a soprano duet the nine voices enter in a conventional polychoral style, balancing alternation and combination of choirs. The harmonic idiom is complex, the slow-moving texture freely decorated with pungent suspensions.

As far as we know, Carissimi's earliest professional experience of church music took place under the maestro in Tivoli, Alessandro Capece, who was employed between 1624 and 1627. This was no bad apprenticeship, since it was one of Capece's most productive periods, judging by the number of his publications in those years. Some ten years before Capece had issued two volumes of Vespers music in a conventional polyphonic idiom,[8] but in his motet collections of 1623 and 1624 he emerged as an exponent of a refreshingly up-to-date *concertato* idiom. His regular approach to rhythmic patterns (crotchet basses and prolonged sections of triple metre) as well as the changing textures of his motets *Quem terra pontus a 7* and *Hodie Christus natus est a 5* must have been noted by Carissimi. The affective style of his Responsories of 1636, which contrast crisp rhythms with daring chromaticism, provides further testimony that this little-known composer was, perhaps, one of the more original musical minds of the century.

Though the small-scale motet as conceived by Roman composers displayed considerable flexibility in its vocal lines, there are some places where the old polyphonic tradition comes to the surface. In *Timete Dominum* (SSATB) the melodic material of the two five-part 'Alleluia' sections is consistently used in conjunction with its own inversion. It is not as if the techniques of the previous generation were ignored; they were simply used sparingly, often in combination with contrasting material. One of the most stylistically homogenous pieces is *Alma redemptoris mater* (SSB), which uses a *basso seguente* and, except for the *tripla*, is consistently polyphonic. The style would have been familiar to Viadana, though the smoothly flowing lines are reminiscent of still earlier models (Ex. 10). In most other pieces the conventional measured pace of the

Ex. 10 (Continuo omitted)

opening soon gives way to more adventurous writing. The setting of a dramatic scriptural passage (Habakkuk, 3: 10–12), *Viderunt te* (SB) shows this technique clearly. After an opening line which has the minim as the basic unit, the words elicit a remarkable series of musical tableaux. 'Abissos' (abysses) has an angular line descending a tenth; 'in luce sagittarum tuarum ibunt' (they went at the flash of your arrows) receives a roulade of semiquavers concluding with an octave leap; on 'furore' (rage) and 'fremitu' (shout) the voices perform protracted semiquaver figurations in parallel tenths; and finally prominent descending sevenths are adopted at 'obstupefacies' (you astound). A similar reminder of polyphonic models at opening sections appears in other works, for instance, the early *O dulcissimum Mariae nomen* (SS); but that of the famous *Laudemus virum gloriosum* (SS) (Ex. 11) of 1656 is more typical of writing later in the century.

Ex. 11 (Continuo omitted)

The constant exchange between the voices in the duet medium was used less frequently during the 1630s, and the two voices were increasingly deployed separately as well as together. Some of Carissimi's works do display an equal partnership of voices, but these are outnumbered by the motets in which the voices tend to function as soloists, uniting to create extra sonority in limited sections. The conventional duet is represented in Carissimi's work by *Anima nostra sustinet* (SS) which is written in four linked sections, the second and fourth of which are in triple metre. Each section, except the last, begins with an extended statement of the material by each voice in turn before they engage in brisker interchange. This increase in momentum is also evident in the halving of the value of the first notes in the first section's incipit when it is repeated. Despite the clear formal scheme of this work, Carissimi does not choose to repeat any material. Elsewhere his works are often unified in this manner, though the motets on the whole exhibit less formal organization than the cantatas. *Exulta gaude* (SS) is a Christmas motet in *ABACAD* form where *A* is a triple-metre duet; here Carissimi varies the ornamentation so that on the second occasion *A* is heard in the manner that an enterprising performer may well have improvised (Ex. 12). The Song of Songs motet *Surgamus eamus* (ATB) is also in refrain form (*ABACADA*) and maintains a quite full texture throughout, except for a series of similes in section *D* which are set as solos. There are

Ex. 12

Ex - ul - ta   gau - - de gau - - de fi - li - a

Ex - ul - ta___ gau - de gau - de fi - li - a

no changes of metre, and the refrain is characterized by the exchange of short rising phrases between all the voices expressing the sense of movement inherent in the text.

Frequently the motets have only a small element of tutti writing. *Hymnum jucunditatis* (SS) contains a middle section of barely overlapping solo phrases, whereas *Sacerdotes Dei* (SS) has extended solos for both voices before concluding in a duet. *O ignis sancte* (SS) has the same form, but here it is cast into sharper relief since, when the voices eventually combine, they do so in a $\frac{6}{4}$ aria style, a striking contrast with the affective recitative which preceded it. One motet is dominated by regular rhythmic writing; after a short introduction *Exurge cor meum* (S, 2 vlns) embarks on a section designated 'aria', a type of movement in quadruple time with a steady crochet bass also found in the works of the Mazzocchis and Foggia. The only interruption in this section is provided by two short related recitatives, and, when these are finished, the five-bar bass pattern is repeated eight times, the voice and instruments performing alternately (Ex. 13). It is more common for Carissimi in his motets to use a strictly rhythmic section as a foil to his characteristically fluid vocal style. For instance, the affective Eucharistic *Ave dulcissime angelorum panis* (SST) is composed of a soprano duet leading into a florid tenor solo and culminating in a strong triple-metre tutti. Here, then, are the roots of the sectionalized style which Carissimi was able to exploit in his dialogue motets.

Standard *ABB* form occurs in a number of motets, such as *Benedictus Deus* (SS). The same procedure is developed in *Desiderata nobis* (ATB), a Christmas motet where the main part of the triple-metre section, 'Iam currite', telling the shepherds of the birth of the Saviour, is repeated to different words, giving a

Ex. 13

De - i pa-rens næ-ro ca-rens pu-ri-ta-te pu-ri-or pro a-mi-cis i-ni-

mi-cis ad - a-mante du-ri-or ad-a-mante du-ri-or

strophic effect. Both 'strophes' open with a phrase sung by each of the voices in turn at a different pitch (starting on D, A, and E), after which the parts combine to develop the same material. *Domine quis habitabit* (SSB) starts by setting the opening of Psalm 14, and it too repeats an entire section of music. After the initial dialogue, in which solo voices answer one another, there is a concluding tutti section, 'O sedes amara', which is marked by a change into triple metre. This final section is sung twice with only minor adaptations to accommodate the upward transposition of a fourth on the second occasion; this is all the more remarkable since the section lasts over twenty bars in a modern edition. *Quomodo facti sunt* (SSB) is unified in a rather different manner since the phrase 'subito defecerunt' acts as a motto throughout the work (Ex. 14). Initially announced in the first soprano, it is taken up on two occasions by the tutti. The opening solo both poses and answers the central question:

Quomodo facti sunt impii in desolatione?

What has happened to the wicked in desolation?

Subito defecerunt, subito perierunt,

They were suddenly eclipsed, they perished suddenly,

Subito aruerunt sicut faenum,

They suddenly burned like hay.

Subito declinaverunt sicut umbra.

They suddenly disappeared like a shadow.

Ex. 14

Su - bi-to de-fe - ce-runt su-bi-to pe-ri - e-runt subi-to a - ru - e-runt sic-ut fae - num

bc

6   43

Su - bi - to de-cli-na - ve - runt   sub-i-to de-cli-na-ve-runt sic-ut   um-bra sic - ut um - bra

6   6   43

Exactly the same musical phrases are then reworked for three voices, a frequent technique in Carissimi's motets; this causes the first repeat of the motto. The same phrase appears again at the very end of the motet, and even at this point the two final crotchets are not lengthened—an effective musical depiction of the wicked passing away as a shadow.

The last two motets discussed both contain some elements of dialogue; one enquires about who shall enter God's presence, the other about the fate of the wicked. Carissimi used changes of texture and scoring to enhance the dramatic effect of these texts; it is in this type of writing (in style at least) that the motet approaches the oratorio. In *Suscitavit Dominus* (ATB) the destruction of Babylon is announced in alto and bass ariosos, after each of which a chorus incites the people to flee and save their souls ('fugite populi'). The tenor then laments the fate of Babylon in another arioso section and the chorus is repeated, this time with the violins, which had previously only supplied *ritornelli*. The person of Christ is characterized in the central arioso of *Timete Dominum* (SSATB) where, after the injunctions to fear the Lord, he extends the invitation, 'Venite ad me omnes qui laboratis' (Come to me all who labour).

The most extended and impressive use of dialogue in Carissimi's motet repertory occurs in *Doleo et poenitet me* (SSTB, 3 viols). To

24

give an idea of the type of texts used in these exchanges, here is the full text of this dialogue, in translation:

God the Father (B): I lament and regret making man; the earth is full of wickedness; I shall destroy everyone from the face of it.

Repentant sinners (SS): O Jesus we cry to you; we beseech you; oh have mercy; oh pray, oh intercede for us to your father.

Christ (T): Father I pray for those who are yours and mine, and you sent me into the world so that they should hear my words and truly know that I came from you and believe that you sent me.

God the Father: I shall wipe out all sinners; depart from me all you workers of wickedness.
Christ: No my father, for I have redeemed them with my precious blood.

Repentant sinners: Woe to us miserable sinners; what shall we do? How shall we escape from the face of the wrath of God? O Jesus, o saviour, intercede for us to your father.

Christ: Father, O most holy father I pray for them; keep them in your grace as I have taken their sins and died for them on the altar of the cross.

God the Father: May they be subdued.

Christ: I do not pray for the world but for them; hear me most holy father for you always listen to me.

Christ: They listen to me, call to me, and those who believe in me come to me for help.
God the Father: You are my beloved son; blessed are those who hear you, and those who believe in you have everlasting life.

Repentant sinners: O Jesus we seek refuge with you, we hear you, we believe you, we appeal to you, we cry to you; grant that we may possess eternal life.

Christ: My father, I have heard these poor sinners who do not cease to cry to me; give them eternal life.

God the Father: I have heard them; I shall give them eternal life.

Repentant sinners: We are converted to the Lord our God since he is God, the good, the merciful, the most pleasant.
Christ: You are converted to the Lord your God since he is God, the good, the merciful, the most pleasant.
God the Father: They are converted to me since I am God, the good, the merciful, the most pleasant.

The motet is written in the arioso style of the oratorios, and its sombre mood is underlined through the use of minor tonality and viol *sinfonie*. In some motets dialogue only plays a secondary role. *Audite sancti* (SSB) sets the rhetorical questions in St Paul's Epistle to the Romans and then supplies them with answers. The original text runs: 'Quis enim separabit a charitate Christi? tribulatio? an angustia? an fames? an nuditas?' (For what shall separate from the love of Christ: tribulation? or difficulty? or hunger? or nakedness?). Carissimi sets the bass against the other voices, which provide the responses (Ex. 15). The opening of the same motet sets the call to

Ex. 15

attention in a bass arioso with rising triadic patterns and uses the characteristic transposition of the initial declamation upon repetition. Exactly the same device opens *Annunciate gentes* (SSATB), a motet with a similar textual incipit. Though set for five voices and divided into seven short movements, the text is not conceived primarily as a dialogue (a few exchanges between the voices occur in the final section). Here Carissimi is using the changes in scoring simply as a musical device:

Section

1	Annunciate gentes	S
2	O quam suavis	SSATB
3	In Domino spes nostra	SS
4	Memorate omnes	AT
5	Omnes adorate Dominum	B
6	Omnes adorate Dominum	SSATB
7	Quid confidistis in potentia?	SSATB

This practice of sectionalization was so characteristic of Roman composers that in the 1620s it was termed 'concertato alla romana' elsewhere in Italy. In this motet it is certainly effective: after the initial declamation, the voices enter in pairs on the weak beats with the exclamation 'O'—a strange device, and one which relies on the continuo to preserve the main pulse. As so often in his works, Carissimi secures a sense of unity by rewriting for the tutti a section previously declaimed by one voice; this happens between sections 5 and 6, where the solo sets out the bass line of the tutti for the first two bars and then provides the motif for subsequent contrapuntal development (Ex. 16). The final section is in the textured *concertato* style; various vocal groupings appear before the tutti, using the same material, brings the movement to a conclusion. This technique is employed in a number of motets, for example the *Salve regina* (SATB, SATB), which relies on a variety of scorings rather than the conventional alternation of choirs.

Solo works account for over an eighth of Carissimi's motet output. *Exurge cor meum*, which has already been discussed, is atypical on account of its regular aria pattern and its use of obbligato instruments. The stylized aria is however found in *Mortalis homo* (S), a contrafactum of the cantata *No, no mio core* (S); since it was published in his lifetime, it seems likely that Carissimi adapted the cantata himself. After a short triple-metre introduction the work is strophic in form; each of the three strophes comprises a section of quadruple metre followed by a song-like *tripla*. The continuo line is repeated for each of the strophes, though slight alterations are made to the voice part to accommodate text and ensure some variety. Such regularity of form is not typical of the motets, neither are the vocal lines generally so lacking in the flexibility characteristic of arioso. This more rigid approach to the

Ex. 16 (Continuo omitted)

om - nes omnes ad - o - ra - te Do - mi - num quo — ni- am

om - nes om-nes   ad-o-ra - te Do -minum ado - ra - te Do - mi - num quo -

om-nes om-nes   ad-o - ra-te Do - mi - num

[-niam]

solo motet is also encountered in the lengthy Marian piece, *O quam pulchra es* (S), in which the extremely virtuosic arioso is interrupted on three occasions by strophes of a simple triple-metre aria (to the same music, but with different words each time). The motet is concluded by three strophes of a further triple-metre aria, 'O virgo benigna', which are performed without any break. It would not be surprising to find that this was another contrafactum, so striking are its similarities with both the style and form of Carissimi's cantatas. The length and extent of virtuoso embellishments in most solo motets suggest that they were intended for performance by a highly trained castrato or falsettist by way of spiritual recreation, rather than in a liturgical context. Certainly published collections of motets from this period, volumes which can safely be regarded as music for church use, contain few examples of the genre. The most dramatic of all Carissimi's essays in this form, *Lucifer caelestis olim* (B), presents the narrative of the Devil's aspirations to rival the glory of God himself; the Almighty responds in no uncertain terms by sending his angels to dispatch Lucifer to the flames of Hell (Ex. 17). Before meeting his demise, Lucifer sings his own praises in two jaunty *tripla* sections, an ironic contrast with the stern *tripla* passage in which judgement is pronounced.

Ex. 17

A less flamboyant use of the solo voice is found in Carissimi's monodic lamentations. His settings of the first two lessons for Holy Thursday survive in a manuscript of Roman provenance devoted to Holy Week music.[9] These pieces represent the closest approach to *parlando* recitative found in Carissimi's sacred music. While the writing is sensitive to the demands of the text and the harmonic style adds an element of pathos, there is none of the melodic inventiveness typical of his arioso style. Flourishes are generally reserved for the introductory Hebrew letters, and in some sections these occur not in the voice but in the continuo (Ex. 18).

The stark atmosphere of the Lamentations represents only one end of the gamut of 'affections' that Carissimi traverses in his music. Perhaps the other extreme is demonstrated in the battle music of *Militia est vita* (SSB), where the *concitato* semiquavers of the vocal parts find a place in the instrumental *ritornelli* as well. The triadic phrases of 'et pugnate cum dracone' (and fight with the dragon) act as a foil to the semiquaver *circulatio* which bears the text 'non coronabitur' (he shall not be crowned). The central

Ex. 18

S — Za - ... in Re-cor-da-ta est Je-

ru - sa-lem di - e - rum af - fli-cti - o - nis su - æ

section is a fiery bass recitative introduced by Carissimi's stock device of beginning a new section a tone below the previous one; the *ritornello* ends on F and the recitative begins, without any preparation, on E^b. Not only warlike texts, commonly found in the works of Jesuit writers, caused Carissimi to respond in a direct, perhaps naïve manner. *Emendemus in melius* (SAT), a penitential motet, introduces short note-values on the word 'subito' (suddenly) after the steady movement of the opening paragraph; there is a prominent diminished fifth at the admission of sin ('peccavimus'), and the tension is raised through ascending semitones at the final cadence. Patterned ornamentation is the response to the words 'Florete flores' (Bloom, you flowers) in *Cantabo Domino* (SS), while a prolonged oscillation between adjacent notes is intended to convey the impression of eternity at 'ad sempiterna' (to eternity) in *Quo tam laetus* (SS). The last named is one of the few motets to employ tempo indications; in exhorting the Christian soldier to share in Christ's suffering, the first part of the phrase is marked 'presto', the remainder 'adagio' (Ex. 19). A number of dynamic marks are found too; the pastoral air of the *tripla* section in the Christmas motet *Desiderata nobis* is heightened by the use of echo at the words 'ut natum videant auctorum saeculi'.

No extended tenure of a post such as Carissimi held at the German College for almost half a century could be without its difficulties. Even a composer and musician of his stature had to

Ex. 19

Va-de va-de fes-ti-na pro-pe-ra ad sup-pli-ci-a ad tor-men-ta ad sup-pli-ci-a ad tor-

-menta ad tormenta ad__ car - ce-res

contend with criticism regarding his failure to teach the students and putti; the employment of too many outsiders; the length of music performed; the behaviour of singers at services; and the amount of money spent on music. By 1657 the stage had been reached where Alexander VII instructed the cardinal protectors of the College to sort out the situation, and they issued a decree dealing with these points. Further general instructions on liturgical music were issued during Carissimi's time as maestro. These documents of 1657 and 1665 emphasized the teaching of the Council of Trent regarding the use of a serious, ecclesiastical style and the banning of secular models. Moreover they forbade the inclusion of long solos and the use of the organ in Passiontide, as well as laying down which texts could be used. Basically it meant that motet texts had to be drawn from appropriate liturgical sources or, during Exposition, from the Fathers or Scripture (with permission); these texts could not be adapted for musical setting. It seems that little attention was paid to these decrees, and that no marked change in Carissimi's motet texts took place in the 1660s. Whatever Carissimi's failings, the College would have been loath to part with a maestro who had brought it such fame for over thirty years.

IV
MUSIC FOR ORATORIES

THE musical genre of the oratorio is popularly linked with the Congregazione dell'Oratorio founded by St Philip Neri during the late sixteenth century as a means of encouraging devotion among the laity. The history of this body is well documented: it arranged meetings away from formal church surroundings (in an oratorio, or prayer-hall) in which sermons in the vernacular and music were heard.[1] By Carissimi's time, however, a prominent venue for such gatherings was the oratorio of the Arciconfraternita del SS Crocifisso. It had nothing to do with St Philip and was a rather different institution: the music was set to Latin texts and the meetings were held on the Fridays of Lent as Lenten exercises for the nobility—a far cry from the daily gatherings organized by St Philip for the edification of the common people of the city. The diarist Ruggieri made mention of the Lenten music in 1650, the first year in which there is evidence that Carissimi participated (he organized the music for the fourth Friday):

Friday, March 11
In the Oratorio of S Marcello [SS Crocifisso] there was superb music in the late evening, and to honour more worthily this event during Holy Year they arranged for some of the Sacred College of Cardinals to preach in person on these holy Fridays which are celebrated so magnificently in the said oratorio . . .[2]

In addition he directed music at the SS Crocifisso in 1658, 1659, and 1660.[3] There were two other meeting places in Rome outside the influence of St Philip's groups, but it seems most unlikely that these used music with Latin texts. There is no evidence that Carissimi was associated with these bodies, which also met during Lent.

It may be affirmed that a Latin oratorio in seventeenth-century Rome is necessarily a work on a Lenten subject. The range of material for vernacular oratorios (of which Carissimi probably wrote two) is wider since the bodies which sponsored them did not confine their activities to Lent. This view of the early Latin oratorio permits us to dispense with traditional categorizations of Carissimi's works; some pieces must now be classed as motets rather than oratorios since the texts were not suitable for performance while the confraternity del SS Crocifisso was meeting, that is, during Lent. The pieces which constitute our revised canon of Carissimi's oratorios are Lenten in different ways, as can be seen from the following table:

Title	Lenten date	Subject/Derivation
Abraham et Isaac	Sunday, week 4	Lesson
Baltazar	Tuesday, week 5	Lesson
Diluvium universale		type of redemption
Historia divitis	Thursday, week 2	Gospel
Ezechia	Thursday after Ash Wednesday	Lesson
Felicitas beatorum/ Damnatorum lamentatio		contrast of good and evil
Jephte		discourse on obedience
Job		discourse on suffering
Jonas	Monday, week 2	Lesson
Judicium extremum	Monday, week 1	Gospel
Judicium Salomonis	Monday, week 4	Lesson
Vanitas vanitatum[4]		transience of existence

The majority of texts is derived from the readings at Mass, while the remainder enunciate the traditional Lenten themes of suffering, obedience, and redemption. The preponderance of Old Testament texts has been frequently discussed; but it simply reflects the substitution of an Old Testament reading for the Epistle on most days of the Lenten season. The view that dialogue motets are the precursors of the Latin oratorio proper is now only partially permissible: composers clearly derived musical elements from these pieces, but the texts are not especially connected with Lenten subjects. Paolo Quagliati's *Ductus est Jesus* (1627), described as a 'dialogo' in the partbooks, is, however, a direct antecedent of the oratorio:[5] the text recounts the temptations of Christ; Satan is personified; and in the concluding tutti he is commanded to depart. Motets for performance during Mass, by Lorenzo Ratti, Carissimi's predecessor at the German College, may well have provided Carissimi with a stylistic model for his oratorios. The large-scale Gospel motet *Homo quidem a 8* is typical of Ratti's style;[6] it recounts the parable of a man who prepared a feast to which his friends were unable to come, and who invited the poor and the sick in their place. The tutti is used to set the scene, to introduce the three excuses of the friends, and to join in a final Alleluia section. A style akin to recitative is used for the dialogue. The vivid nature of Lenten texts encouraged the development of a dramatic oratorio style; no similar settings would have been produced with the reflective, theological language of the Epistles as a basis. Carissimi's contact with Francesco Manelli, singer and maestro at Tivoli and future composer of Venetian opera, must have taught him something about maximizing the dramatic impact of libretti. Though no extended works of Manelli's from this period are known, it is hard to believe that he had not already gained some of the feel for setting narrative to music which was to make him so successful in Venice.

Throughout these works Carissimi directs his energies towards securing the greatest possible sense of drama. This he does through arranging the text into well-constructed tableaux. In *Jephte* three can be discerned: the battle; victory celebrations; and laments. Carissimi concentrates on unifying individual sections and building up their atmosphere, and the dramatic effect is the product of the juxtaposition of strongly defined contrasting sections. To gain victory in battle Jephthah vows that he will sacrifice the first creature he sees on returning home; he wins, his daughter runs out to greet him, and immediately their lamentations commence. The victory celebrations are a cohesive unit: they consist of two soprano solos separated by a soprano duet, and followed by a six-part chorus. Apart from the internal unity of the musical phrases—the result of Carissimi's propensity for transposition—there are other means of unification. The duet takes its triple metre from the central section of the first solo, and it is internally compact in that it comprises only two phrases both of which are immediately transposed by one step. The final section of the first solo provides melodic material for the second solo, the words and rhythm of which are passed directly to the chorus. The tonal basis of G major, so thoroughly established, is an effective foil to the anguished A minor of the laments—the abrupt tonal change increases the emotional power of the moment, as does the entry of a solitary voice after the spirited tutti section. Carissimi then continues to unify the lament section using similar methods:

the A minor tonality is a significant point of reference; Jephthah's monodies incorporate the music of his initial utterance 'Heu, heu mihi!'; and his daughter's plaint is structured around echo effects, as the mountains reply to her distress.

Elsewhere in his oratorios Carissimi approaches the crucial moment of the drama with equal skill. As Isaac is on the point of being sacrificed in *Historia di Abraham et Isaac* his ignorance of his fate is emphasized by the way he sings blandly in a major tonality to ask about the identity of the sacrificial victim. The tragic minor-key duet of father and son ensues; in this, arguably the finest example of the rhetorical device of *suspiratio* in Carissimi's work, the composer even uses rests in the middle of words (Ex. 20). When the sense of gloom has been fully evoked, and Abraham has stretched out his hand to kill the boy, the narrator's part suddenly rises through an octave on the words 'Angelus Domini de caelo clamans'; the unexpected shift to a major tonality reflects the transformation of the situation through divine intervention. In *Baltazar*, when Daniel interprets the writing on the wall, the tension is heightened by introducing each succeeding word a tone higher than the previous one; this is particularly effective since the tonal centre A, that of the final word, had already been associated in the oratorio with the concept of mystery.

The ideal of structural cohesion, noted in *Jephte*, is pursued by Carissimi in his other works. *Historia di Job* is punctuated by a refrain 'Sit nomen Domini benedictum' (Blessed be the name of the Lord), whose frequency is clearly intended to symbolize the constancy of Job in the face of suffering. He breaks into this triple-metre statement after each of the answers he gives to the Devil's announcement of his misfortunes. The refrain is also worked into the final trio in which minor textual variants help reflect the individual feelings of each character. Towards the end the Devil's part finishes, leaving the Angel and Job singing together. In a short work such as *Job* there is little room for the tableau forms of *Jephte*; it is, in fact, a single unit in which the final rejoicing grows out of the continuing praise of God during the piece. This is not the case in *Abraham et Isaac*, where the concluding song of praise is at variance with the general atmosphere of the work. It is a well-wrought movement in *ABA* form, where the *B* section is a triple-metre interjection dominated by the Angel and Abraham. The first time *A* is heard it cadences in C major, and the second time the conclusion is on G, *A* having been transposed with appropriate

Ex. 20

adjustments. Even this set piece is not unrelated to the rest of the work, since the opening phrase 'Omnes populi' is derived from the preceding passage for the Angel.

If it can be considered an oratorio, *Vanitas vanitatum* is certainly the most tightly structured example in Carissimi's output. The text is a meditation on the transience of human existence, so it does not impose the same restrictions as a narrative on the formal structure. The theme of the work becomes centred in the choruses (all

36

similar in style), which are repeated as interlocking refrains; interleaved with these, several voices sing meditations on the ephemeral nature of life:

T C S C A C B C S C SS ATB C

C signifies chorus; the other letters refer to voices

In his other oratorios Carissimi constructs self-contained sections to reinforce a particular element in the action. In *Ezechia*, the protagonist's prayer is a set piece, comprising three sections, each of which is answered by an instrumental *sinfonia* (the first two *sinfonie* are identical). Each petition concludes with an identical setting of the words 'parce mihi, Domine' (spare me, o Lord). The same structure, in this case perhaps reflecting the three persons of the Godhead, is used in Jonah's prayer from the belly of the whale. There is no final *ritornello*, but the refrain in each section, 'Placare, Domine', demonstrates characteristic economy of material; it comprises two phrases, both of which are immediately transposed up a fourth (*AA'BB'*). In *Judicium extremum* the central idea of the dead being raised to judgement is underscored by recalling the duet 'Surgite mortui' after two recitative sections; the duet is also transposed by a fourth at the repeat, so that it not only frames the section but also creates a sense of moving on to the following one.

Another use of repetition within a section occurs in *Baltazar*; here the feasting and merry-making are centred on G major, after which the writing on the wall is announced by the Historicus in C major. The banquet comprises seven parts (after which the instruments are silent until the final chorus):

1 S, 2 vlns	Inter epulas
2 SSATB, 2 vlns	Regi nostro complaudamus
3 Short *sinfonia*, 2 vlns	
4 SSATB, 2 vlns	Curae tristes procul este
5 S, 2 vlns	Hic dum floret nobis aetas
6 A, 2 vlns	Procul maestus eat questus
7 SS, 2 vlns	Regi nostro complaudamus

The first five sections form a kind of arch: 'Inter epulas' is the same as 'Hic dum floret' in all respects except for the text; and the two tutti movements are similar in structure except that a different voice plays a prominent role in the reduced passages. The final duet, 'Regi nostro complaudamus', recalls the words of the first

37

chorus. Individual sections are compact: 'Inter epulas', for example, consists of three phrases, each followed by its transposition, and a brief coda; and 'Procul maestus' adopts a similar pattern, though rather less strictly. Similarly, the duet 'Regi nostro complaudamus' can be represented $ABCA'B'C'AD$, where $A'B'C'$ represent transposed versions and D is a derivative of C. The most powerful application of these procedures appears in *Judicium extremum* where the entire 'judgement' section is framed by massive choruses ('Quam magna') for eleven voices and instruments, commenting on the terror of the sentence. Here the intention may well have been twofold; the repeated chorus not only gives a satisfactory conclusion to the oratorio in a musical sense, but also provides an opportunity for the people to echo the sentiments of the souls raised to judgement. Carissimi seems to have been motivated by textual considerations in his choice of the SSATB/ATB/ATB scoring, since ATB groups are used to represent righteous and sinners respectively; their incorporation into the larger texture is surely planned to illustrate the universality of the day of reckoning.

The eleven-part choruses of *Judicium extremum* demonstrate an aspect of the peculiarly Roman 'colossal Baroque' style; they are very similar to psalm-settings from Virgilio Mazzocchi's 1648 publication.[7] 'Tunc horibili sonitu' exhibits *concertato* deployment of voices: the movement is introduced by a solo tenor, and later a number of duets for various voices punctuate the brisk, rhythmically decisive exchange between the choirs. The relative scarcity of tutti writing makes this chorus more typical of the Roman Baroque than the other, 'Quam magna'. Similar writing is used to considerable effect for the powerful evocation of the storm in *Jonas*: the relentless dotted rhythms, with each choir's phrases dovetailing into the other's, develop a considerable momentum. In this instance the choir stands in the place of a narrator to describe the storm; but Carissimi also uses choruses as participants in the action (those present at the feast in *Baltazar*), and also, like the chorales in Bach's Passions, to represent the church. The active choruses of demons in *Historia divitis* contain some of Carissimi's most effective choral writing. He shows a more flexible use of *concertato* textures than usual; there is even some eight-part counterpoint which provides an effective build-up at 'et mille mille malis' in 'Iam satis edisti'. But some of the later choruses are even more remarkable for their gloomy, threatening, and endless repetition of the word 'morere' (die) in near-homophony. 'Igneas tartari fornaces' is a well-wrought section: the voice of Dives (T) asks questions about hell to which the remainder of the eight-part choir responds until interrupted by the bass voice singing 'Descende nobiscum . . . in aeternum', a chant which is taken up by the tutti (Ex. 21). The chorus is cast in the role of the church at

Ex. 21

De - scen - de no - bis-cum in in-fer-num in in - fer - num u - bi

u - bi es cru-ci-an-dus u - bi   u - bi es cru-ci-an-dus in ae- ter-num in ae-ter-num in ae -

ter-num in ae - ter - num

the end of *Ezechia*, where the text 'Narrabimus omnes opera' praises the works of God. *Abraham et Isaac* and *Judicium Salomonis* conclude in the same way, while *Jonas* culminates in a chorus of penitence—a sentiment appropriate to Lent, but also the response of the people of Nineveh to Jonah's preaching.

Carissimi often moulds the vocal texture so that it recalls the grand *concertato* style of the early part of the century; but the reduced sections and the tutti are not generally dovetailed as they are in the works of his older contemporaries. 'Curae tristes' from

39

Baltazar is a chorus for five voices, yet the role of the tutti simply lies in repeating the last few words of each line of the bass part homophonically, thus defining a regular pattern of textures. Even in the final moralizing chorus of *Judicium Salomonis* the tutti is used polyphonically in the latter half. In the opening section of this, however, the chordal tutti writing is interleaved with duets for the two sopranos (Ex. 22). It seems that, by the 1640s, the earlier ideal

Ex. 22 (Violins omitted)

of constantly changing textures had given way to a conventional formula—the regular alternation of certain voices or a group of voices with the tutti. This is analogous to the increasingly systematic approach to rhythm and structure found during this period.

There has been much discussion about the nature of the chorus in Carissimi's oratorios: is it a separate group from the soloists, do the soloists form part of it, or is it in many cases simply the solo parts combined? Unfortunately records of payment to musicians cease after 1623 at the SS Crocifisso. Mortoft, visiting the SS Crocifisso in 1659, noted that on one occasion a dozen singers performed, and on another at least twenty.[8] Perhaps he was given to slight exaggeration, for it does seem curious that in so many of Carissimi's oratorios the number and the voices of the soloists correspond to those of the chorus:

Oratorios	Soloists	Chorus
Abraham et Isaac	SATTB	SATTB
Baltazar	SSATB	SSATB
Diluvium universale	survives incomplete	
Historia divitis	STTB	SATB; SATB
Ezechia	SSATB	SSATB
Felicitas beatorum/ Damnatorum lamentatio	—	SSS/ATB
Jephte	SSSATB	SSSATB
Job	SAB	SAB
Jonas	SATTBB	SATB;SATB
Judicium extremum	ATB; ATB; SSTB	ATB; ATB; SSATB
Judicium Salomonis	SSAB	SSAB
Vanitas vanitatum	SSATB	SSATB

If the large forces mentioned by Mortoft were present anyway, this would seem to make the careful organization of voices unnecessary. However, Carissimi could have planned them in this manner to render optional the extra forces available at the SS Crocifisso on Lenten Fridays. In doing this he was ensuring that the oratorios could also be performed at smaller devotional gatherings or services, perhaps at the German College. This could also well account for the circulation of some pieces with and without instrumental parts.

Not all of Carissimi's ensembles demand the tutti scorings; much of his most interesting writing is found in small-scale groupings. The three-part section which concludes *Job* is exceptional, since the third voice, representing the Devil, drops out—a symbol of his defeat. In the same oratorio Job interjects the words 'Audio, audio' in the message of the first misfortune, thus weakening the form of the set-piece monody (Ex. 23). Small

ensembles are commonly used to depict characters in the drama. Vocal writing in the duet of the women in *Judicium Salomonis* is deliberately unorthodox in order to reflect the heated argument; there is close imitation with abrupt phrase endings and sudden interjections. The three-part ensembles for sailors in *Jonas* also portray real speech: in 'Judica nobis' Carissimi singles out individual voices to ask Jonah each question (Ex. 24)—and the discussion about his fate elicits some imitative writing. In the sailors' invocation to their gods, 'Dii magni', rising anxiety is reflected in the sequential repetitions of the exclamations (on A, C, D, and finally F). Similar transpositions also occur in *Vanitas vanitatum*, where an ATB ensemble enumerates the worthless trappings of worldly glory which will pass away. Here the tonal bases are F, G, A, C, D, and F; the sequence starts with the two lowest voices and concludes with the two highest, the scoring following the rise in pitch.

    Judicium extremum also includes some three-voice ensembles of righteous and sinners. The use of one voice set against the other

Ex. 24

two in the sinners' ensemble 'Domine, quando te vidimus' could, to the seventeenth-century mind, have symbolized the enmity among the damned. This contrasts with the smooth, unified counterpoint given to the believers in their ensemble. That Carissimi was not averse to using deliberate symbolism is clear from the SS duet, 'Et reversus est' in *Ezechia*, a passage which describes the sun being turned back in its course; the soprano parts depict the notion of 'reversus' by abandoning their customary parallel thirds (Ex. 25). Despite the skilful treatment of the chorus and ensemble sections, it is monody which carries the main thrust of the oratorio plots. Carissimi does not always confine the narration to one voice within an oratorio: for instance, in *Jephte* soprano, alto, and bass voices are used (the tenor voice is reserved for the character of Jephthah himself); and in *Baltazar* the soprano, alto, and tenor are used, Baltazar being represented by a bass soloist.

Ex. 25 (Continuo omitted)

There is one other place within the dramatic structure which is given to the solo voice, albeit exceptionally. Just as the chorus occasionally takes the role of narrator, the solo voice can comment on the action, as it does at the end of *Judicium extremum* with the words 'O vox tristis et funesta'—a reflection (using the rhetorical device of *climax*) on the awesomeness of the voice of Christ pronouncing judgement (Ex. 26). In scoring the oratorio texts

Ex. 26

Carissimi has none of the inhibitions which caused other composers to set the words of Christ as a duet. The hidebound religious atmosphere which forced Cavalieri, for instance, to choose a moral subject in order to avoid the representation of saints and the persons of the Trinity, was a thing of the past. In *Abraham et Isaac* the Patriarch is addressed directly by God (not through a narrator); and in *Judicium extremum* Christ personally delivers the sentence.

In setting the words of individuals Carissimi is at his most sensitive, and probably for this reason the monodies of his oratorios are the most widely discussed parts of his work. We have considered his treatment of the depth of Abraham's anguish as he is about to sacrifice Isaac, but an examination of the specifically musical techniques he uses at these crucial moments is instructive. A comparison of the reactions of the two women in *Judicium Salomonis*, when Solomon decides to cut the disputed child in half, shows how Carissimi goes beyond the text to distinguish their attitudes (Ex. 27). The passage sung by the first woman uses major

Ex. 27

tonalities: there seems to be no hint of grief, only a studied nonchalance which persists until the word 'dividatur' is painted with considerable impact and almost relish. In contrast the second woman's part is set in minor tonalities, the rest is used to highlight the sigh, and the vocal line falls to dissonances on words referring to her child. Later the word 'dividatur' is not singled out with any anticipatory musical divisions, and the chromatic bass line rises—a device frequently associated with distress. Carissimi's penchant for portraying the human situation is not restricted to occasions of despair. Later in the same oratorio, the woman whose child has been restored to her breaks into a miniature aria in quadruple metre, quite distinct from her plaintive recitatives; in 'Congratulamini omnes' the vocal line assumes a new vitality and the bass line loses its static quality. The transposition of phrases of regular length gives the section a certain momentum which differs greatly from the looser rhythmical structure of the recitative writing. The use of triple-metre arias to contrast with recitative is already clearly defined in Carissimi's oratorios; it appears much like a cameo of later manifestations of the style. At the beginning of *Job* the Angel sings a well-balanced passage in this form to the words 'Spiritus malus est'.

Carissimi occasionally unifies a number of related sections by writing strophic arias. 'En vitae suprema' from *Historia divitis* is an example of this: there are three triple-time sections on the same bass line, each culminating in a short *sinfonia*. The vocal line is virtually the same in each section apart from some details of embellishment. The relative scarcity of strophic forms in Carissimi's oratorios is not surprising, as they almost never occur in Roman church music. None the less this marks a difference from secular music, which in Rome was dominated by strophic variations, at least early in the century. Carissimi, an enthusiast for well-defined forms, finds other ways of organizing song-like passages, which on the whole are insufficiently extended to require complex formal procedures. At moments of rising tension he was not opposed to abrupt changes of tonality (as at the sailors' invocations in *Jonas*). At 'Sat mensas mille' in *Historia divitis* he organizes a succession of song-like passages in this manner, a scalic melody rising through a fifth at the beginning acting as a head-motif. The five sections, on the tonal centres F, G, A, C, and D, are shared between the soprano and tenor voices, and each gives a different reason why Dives deserves the punishment that awaits him. The climax of this section is reached when the soprano pronounces judgement, 'Ubi ab igne voraberis', on a single note in triple metre; as if to bring home the point, the whole section is then repeated one tone lower. A similar use of varied tonality occurs, as we have seen, in the interpretation of the mysterious writing on the wall in *Baltazar*. Often, clear formal structures in the solos emerge from Carissimi's interest in repetition and transposition as rhetorical devices: the 'Plorate colles' section of the daughter's lament in *Jephte* marks out *AA'BB'* form (two phrases with transposed repetition), while the 'Plorate, plorate, filii Israel' section is *ABB'*, with the *B* phrase brought back a fifth lower. *ABB'* form appears, too, in the first section of *Baltazar*; here the line of text repeated is central to the plot.

It would seem unlikely that Carissimi was, in these brief movements, aiming to construct a particular form; rather, his preoccupation probably lay in the recall of the most crucial phrases for emphasis. Although, as Smither has remarked, the da capo structure is not strictly found in the oratorios,[9] some foreshadowing of it is seen in the insertion of central triple sections in, for instance, the daughter's song of rejoicing in *Jephte* ('Incipite in tympanis') and the opening recitative of *Baltazar*. A more clearly defined use of the form is apparent in the duet of father and son in *Abraham et Isaac*, where triple-time sections flank the central quadruple one.

In his solo sections Carissimi is mainly concerned with the details of the text. As well as creating a general impression of mood through choice of tonality and speed of declamation (almost halting altogether for sighs), he tends to single out certain words for a more graphic portrayal. Some devices appear again and again: the rest for sighs (*suspiratio*); and the triadic motifs for battle in *Jephte*, and for the dead returning to life and the trumpet calls in *Judicium extremum*. Jonah and Isaiah are both bidden with rising chordal motifs to go and speak the word of the Lord. The notions of falling and descent are treated in an analogous manner: when Dives is informed of the nature of hell in *Historia divitis* the bass voice at 'Igneas tartari fornaces' drops to a low D—a setting comparable to the depiction of the abyss in Monteverdi's *Ab aeterno* (1640). Portions of text in *Judicium extremum* receive similar treatment, such as at the words 'haedos autem a sinistris' (but the goats to the left) and 'in profundum' (into the depths); by contrast, the words 'in aera' (in the air) have a floating phrase, echoed by the violins. A more gentle, chromatic descent is reserved for the woman falling to the ground to praise Solomon for returning her child in *Judicium Salomonis*. In the same oratorio there are some less obvious instances of word-painting: the oscillation between two notes in Solomon's part at the word 'discernere' (discern) is meant to convey indecision, while at 'Dividite infantem' (divide the child) the beat is broken into smaller rhythmic units, and the form used is *AABB*, where *B* is a transposition of *A*. Another division of notes appears for quite a different reason at the words 'dolentes' (sorrowing) and 'gementes' (crying) in *Historia divitis*: the vocal line almost approaches the *trillo*, a common seventeenth-century musical device associated with grief. More picturesque, fanciful figures are found in *Abraham et Isaac*, where a rambling, dotted-note phrase illustrates Isaac being tied to the altar; the same idea turns up in *Jonas* to portray the whale swallowing, and eventually vomiting the protagonist (Ex. 28).

Ex. 28

Et pre-pa - ra - vit Do-mi-nus cetum grandem   ut de - glu - ti - ret Jo - nam

Instrumental parts—two treble instruments and an occasional *basso istrumentale*—appear in all the Latin oratorios with the exception of *Abraham et Isaac, Jephte*, and the miniature *Job*. Their use to highlight a particular section of *Baltazar* (the banquet) has already been noted. Archival records of the SS Crocifisso provide evidence of their use, at least from 1664, when a series of documents relating to payments begins.[10] However, a list of musicians during Lent at the Oratorio of the Arciconfraternita dell'Orazione e Morte, dating from 1618, mentions two cornetti, two violins, violone, lute, theorbo, cembalo, and organ;[11] one can be certain that the SS Crocifisso with its fine reputation would not have been outdone by ensembles such as these. While their most characteristic role is to fill out the texture in choruses, Carissimi also uses instruments to provide short *sinfonie* and occasionally to echo the vocal line in aria-like passages. Apart from *Historia divitis*, all the oratorios to include instrumental parts open with a short *sinfonia*. The most developed of these is perhaps the one which opens *Judicium Salomonis*: it comprises two sections, the first in quadruple metre and the second in triple. The two violins play duets in thirds and sixths over the bass, and the style is far from complex. One oratorio, *Historia divitis*, uses a *sinfonia* as a type of refrain: a short section of repeated chords in a *concitato* style is heard five times, that is, after most of the tutti sections. Carissimi's concern for cohesion is very marked in this, his longest oratorio: two choruses enclose, and one acts as the central pivot for the section leading up to Dives' death—this is where his fate is decided and the terrors of hell are described. These sections all conclude with the same extended passage which leads to the *sinfonia*. Independent instrumental parts were not frequently found in Roman church music; even though the parts in Carissimi's oratorios are not particularly interesting, it is striking that they are there at all.

Spagna, the first historian of the oratorio, comments on the context of the genre in the services at the SS Crocifisso; this prompts an examination of this aspect of Carissimi's Latin works. He notes that originally two unrelated oratorios were included in a service, whereas later more extended bipartite works were composed, so that the same subject was musically presented before and after the sermon. The original type can best be represented by *Job* and *Abraham et Isaac*, whereas *Judicium extremum* and *Historia divitis* must fall into the latter category. This theory is supported by the fact that both oratorios have a natural point of division: the former could be adjourned before or after the chorus 'Quam magna' depending on whether it was thought better to end each half with the same music or to make a symmetrical second half, beginning and ending with the chorus. *Historia divitis* reaches a convenient break after the chorus 'Igneas tartari fornaces'; the second portion then begins immediately with the death of Dives. In this respect, according to Spagna, the Latin oratorio came to resemble the Italian form, and it is the place of the *oratorio volgare* in Carissimi's output that we shall now consider.

The English traveller Mortoft provides evidence of Carissimi's association with the Oratorians in their church, the Chiesa Nuova,[12] and this links him with the tradition of oratorio in the vernacular:

... Afterward wee went to the Chiesa Nova, where wee heard that never enough to be praised and delightful Musicke. The subject was made by A Prince of Rome and Composed by Charissima, who for that is accounted the best in the world ... all which made so sweete a harmony, that never the like must againe be expected, unlesse in heaven and in Rome.

Mortoft's remarks demonstrate that oratorio texts were not simply translated from the Vulgate; that the author was a 'Prince of Rome' fits the idea of a vernacular libretto. Italian oratorios do not figure greatly in Carissimi's output; in fact, Massenkeil (in *New Grove*) regards the two works to be discussed here as doubtful or misattributed. None the less it is clear that our composer was associated with the Oratorian order (if only slightly), and for that reason some examples of the vernacular oratorio merit consideration. These works can also bring into greater relief the study of the Latin oratorio.

The libretto of *Daniele* is based on the plot to have him thrown into the lion's den, and though it follows the accepted two-section structure of the *oratorio volgare*, the work does not reach a satisfactory dramatic conclusion. The final chorus is a demand for Daniel's death sung by the satraps. Musically the style is rather different from that of Carissimi's Latin works: the recitative is more simple; some of the choruses are more truly contrapuntal; and the aria sections are more distinctive, and merge less with the recitative. Differences in style can partially be attributed to the fact that here the composer is working with a different kind of text—a poetic one, rather than one in prose. The natural rhyme scheme and structure of the texts militate against the introduction of rhetorical conventions used in his settings of Latin prose: frequent repetitions would confuse the form of the poetry, and the metrical layout itself renders other, musical means of organization redundant.

In *Daniele* Carissimi follows the practice of the Latin oratorios in combining the solo voices to produce tutti. Both sections end with a chorus, and a further one appears in the first half; all these ensembles represent the satraps. There is some sense of musical cohesion where the chorus 'No, no, non fia vera, si scacci' takes up the material just sung by the third satrap; the opening cries of 'no' elicit a fragmented texture—an isolated attempt on Carissimi's part to inject into this work some of the dramatic sense of the Latin pieces (Ex. 29). Perhaps the most interesting chorus is that which concludes the first half, 'Dario, non più s'indugi'. In six parts, it displays a contrapuntal, almost madrigalian style virtually absent from the chordal ensembles of the Latin works. The texture is in a continual state of transformation. Two phrases dominate the movement, a falling one for 'dona a morte Daniele' (put Daniel to death) and a more animated one characterized by the rise of a fourth at 'guerra, guerra' (war, war); eventually the latter idea takes over. The chorus which ends the second half is a simple homophonic movement in triple metre; the six-part choir is divided into two groups (SSS and ATB), and these maintain a dialogue.

Triple-metre arias are more prominent in this than in any other

Ex. 29 (Continuo omitted)

of Carissimi's oratorios. Daniel's first section comprises a passage of simple recitative which leads to a tuneful triple-metre aria at 'Gl'imperi più grandi'. This is arranged in three strophes, all of which are in *ABB'* form (where *B'* is *B* transposed up a tone). The bass remains the same throughout the three sections, but the embellishment of the vocal melody varies. Darius follows this with an aria 'Sì, sì, son degni di te' and the three satraps then expound their attitude towards Daniel in arias, the first of which is in quadruple metre, the second in *ABB* form. Daniel has a second aria, 'Hor chi sospende destra irate?', in the second half; again the short final phrase is repeated in what has clearly by now become the conventional manner.

The *Oratorio della SS Vergine* is similar to *Daniele* in matters of musical style: Carissimi uses the same simple recitative idiom, and also introduces a madrigalian chorus. Bianchi suggests that the Marian piece is an early work.[13] The two Italian oratorios are certainly rather different in conception from the Latin pieces, and seem to lack their internal unity and polished style. This may lead us to speculate whether Carissimi was involved with the Oratorian order before he formed his connections with the SS Crocifisso; the fact that the text of the *Oratorio della SS Vergine* is Marian may be significant, since the main Oratorian church in Rome is dedicated to the Virgin, S Maria in Vallicella. The text, by the poet Francesco Balducci, reflects on the triumph of the Virgin, the second Eve, over the serpent. Mary is the only character in the piece; the other voices act as anonymous devotees. Foreshadowing the quietism of the latter half of the *Seicento,* this oratorio is far removed from the matter-of-fact approach of the Latin oratorio. Though the subject matter is not as fanciful, *Vanitas vanitatum* is the Latin work which most closely resembles this piece. Both are meditative rather than dramatic (though the Virgin's conflict with the serpent is briefly described); recurrent musical devices become important in engendering the sense of cohesion that a continuing plot would otherwise provide. Smither has made some pertinent comments on recurring bass patterns in the *Oratorio della SS Vergine*;[14] this phenomenon would suggest an early date of composition, since stock basses fell into a rapid decline after the mid-1620s. Further means of tying the several sections of the oratorio together are also found: the part designated in the libretto as the 'proem' comprises three verses; these are set as soprano duets separated by *sinfonie*. The Virgin's three main recitatives in the first half all conclude with the same phrase, 'né senza me fora', which is repeated at a different pitch. Another solo voice responds to these statements of the Virgin's position within the created order; and, as if to emphasize that Mary is on a different existential plane, other solo passages avoid the F major tonality which is reserved for her. In this connection it is interesting to note that the first half ends in B^b, giving the entire oratorio a binary structure.

For the most part the recitatives are simply unembellished presentations of the text. Some word-painting does occur: in the proem words like 'ridea' (laughed) and 's'indorava' (gilded itself) are lightly ornamented, and where the Virgin speaks of her predestination ('Io dell'eterna Mente') there is a low monotone at 'fondamenti' (foundations). The most animated vocal writing occurs when the bass narrates the victory over the serpent at 'Lasciava il fero in suo sentiero'; the voice part descends at the mention of 'Valle' (valley); and a remote E^b tonality is introduced at the dramatic words which describe the progress of evil 'Tra le sue spire chiudeansi i monti . . .' (Between its [the serpent's] coils the mountains close in on themselves). Eventually her victory over the monster is announced with a brisk melisma and a return to F major. At this moment the celebrations of her triumph commence in a pastoral vein: there are two ATB ensembles linked together by the repetition of a prolonged closing section. This section is strongly reminiscent of the secular pastoral mode; but for what has preceded it, we could be witnessing the merry-making of the nymphs and shepherds in an Arcadian vision.

The work contains two choruses, one at the end of each half.

The first, 'Ecco al vento', has three identical musical sections, with only the text changing. In these the duetting sopranos present material which is repeated in a harmonized version by the other voices, and with the violins adding some extra substance. The recall to prominence of the two sopranos gives the section a balanced, rounded form. 'Notte mai non è sì nera' is unashamedly madrigalian; after a homophonic statement of the first line of text the voices explore the contrapuntal possibilities of the phrase 'doppo il verno i prati' until at the very end they unite in homophony.

Although Carissimi did not initiate the genre as some have claimed, he was intimately associated with the institutions where the oratorio was cultivated at an early stage in its development. His contribution lies in bringing a sensitive dramatic aspect to the sectionalized forms already well established in Rome. His dramatic ability and his capacity for delineating the affects were much admired by his contemporaries. But his reputation reached wider areas: as we shall see, both French and German composers were radically influenced by his achievements in this field.

V
THE CANTATA

SINCE Carissimi's name has generally been associated with church music, it may be surprising to learn that his contribution to the cantata represents the most prolific side of his output. About 150 survive, mostly in manuscripts which provide scant information on poets, circumstances of composition, or dates. Almost all the solo pieces, three-quarters of his cantata output, are for soprano and continuo, while the remainder are for two and three voices in a ratio of three to one. There is no standard form, and while much of the verse is anonymous, it largely reflects the legacy of Giambattista Marino, the foremost exponent of lyric poetry in the early *Seicento.*

Though the term 'cantata' was first used by Alessandro Grandi in a volume of music dating from shortly before 1620,[1] where it was applied to strophic variations, it soon became used to refer to the whole spectrum of vocal music with Italian texts. While Rome was the centre of cantata composition, it is difficult to trace the development of the genre there since most of the repertory survives not in prints but undated manuscripts. By the time Carissimi produced his first cantatas, two strands seem to have been established within the genre: the *arietta corta*, or self-contained aria; and the *aria a più parti*, a composite work comprising a number of sections in different styles. It is a mark of his contribution to the growing sophistication of the genre that Carissimi favoured the latter, more complex type.

One can imagine that his interest in secular music received a considerable upturn after his appointment as 'Maestro di Cappella del concerto di camera' to Christine of Sweden in July 1656, a position he won on account of his 'evident merits and the perfection which he enjoys in his practice of music'.[2] Mortoft witnessed the chamber music at Christine's palazzo in January 1659: '. . . Wee saw her in her chamber converse with many Gentlemen that came to heare Musicke that night. It being her custome every Wensday night to have the best Muscitianers at her

Pallace, she being much delighted in Musicke.'[3] A number of Carissimi's cantatas can be provided with *termini ad quem* before his appointment to Christine's court, through references in letters or, occasionally, through publications. Though he was involved with the Barberini household as a teacher of counterpoint in the mid-1630s, there is no evidence of his producing music for performance there. Indeed it is possible that his two earliest datable cantatas were the product of a rather different area of patronage: *Fuggi quel ben* (AT), published 1640, and *Alma che fai* (SB), of two years later, belong to the handful of cantatas which have spiritual texts. Their allegorical, moralizing tone might suggest a connection with the Oratorio of St Philip Neri: the former deals with the need to flee worldly delights in pursuit of lasting heavenly pleasures, while the latter is a dialogue of body and soul reminiscent of the *lauda* text which plays a central role in Cavalieri's famous *Rappresentatione*. These compositions are untypical of Carissimi's cantatas in a number of other respects: the duet medium used in both pieces accounts for only about a sixth of his works, and thus neither the monodic dialogue which begins *Alma che fai* nor the contrapuntal interplay of voices is characteristic of the cantatas.

A further eight spiritual cantatas survive, including one of particular interest because it sets a text by Flavio Chigi, later Pope Alexander VII. *Nella più verde età* (S, 2 vlns) is one of the few cantatas to introduce string *ritornelli*; it is a lengthy piece in which conventional pastoral imagery is the basis for a meditation on the inevitability of suffering. The contrast between the declamatory writing, often verging on arioso, and the triple-time aria style is an essential feature of this, as of many more extended cantatas; yet Carissimi was not satisfied with simple contrast but sought to give the work an overall shape. Starting with simple declamation and moving towards his characteristic arioso style, he soon introduces the first of the aria sections in $\frac{3}{8}$ time. The central aria section, by way of contrast, is a $\frac{6}{4}$ piece, giving the cantata an *ABA* form. His preferred pattern, however, is *ABB'*—also common in the oratorios —which appears in two guises in most sections of the work:

$$\tfrac{3}{8}\,abb' \,\|\, \tfrac{4}{4}\,cc' = \tfrac{3}{8}\,A\,\tfrac{4}{4}\,BB'$$

On each occasion the repeat is transposed but other alterations are few. Carissimi loses no opportunity for underscoring the text.

Some of Carissimi's most dramatic writing is found in the

spiritual cantatas, particularly in his settings of the poet Domenico Benigni. *Suonerà l'ultima tromba* (S) warns of the impending last judgement, and, like the previous piece, it combines a complex structure with remarkable economy of material:

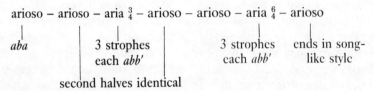

In this, one of his lengthiest cantatas, Carissimi runs the gamut of word-painting, from the bold oscillations of the 'ultima tromba' to the tranquil descending scale on the last line which states, 'Though Heaven may rouse him with grievous warnings, he, oppressed with the torpor of vices, sleeps on'. An animated scene is also depicted in the two cantatas on the theme of battle, in praise of the noble Roman family of the Savelli. The opening of *Che magnanimi heroi* (S) sets the tone for the whole cantata, though even the opening melisma on 'tromba' (Ex. 30) is dwarfed by the one which appears

on the words 'gonfia la tromba' (blow the trumpet) later in the work. The whole work is a song in praise of heroism, presented in an exaggerated poetic and musical style; the final climax proclaims that nothing can obscure the noble deeds of the family, and is reached through particularly bold gestures (Ex. 31).

Ex. 31

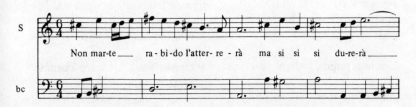

Non mar-te____ ra - bi-do l'atter- re - rà   ma si si si   du-re-rà____

These works are far removed from the main corpus of Carissimi's cantatas which, predictably enough, have unrequited love as their subject matter. Most are written in the first person and lament the cruelty of the beloved. The earliest secular cantatas of Carissimi's which can safely be dated are two from *Ariette di musica* published in Bracciano, near Rome, in 1646. One is a two-voiced dialogue and the other a solo cantata, *Chi d'amor vive in tormento* (S). The anonymous text of this short cantata is a good example of the type of subject favoured by Carissimi for compositions in this genre:

Chi d'amor vive in tormento,	Whoever lives tormented by love,
senza mai cangiar desire,	never changing his desires,
speri un dì lieto e contento	may hope one day in happiness and contentment
di dar finir al suo martire.	to end his suffering.
Se non è di selce un Alma,	If it is not made of flint, a soul
a pietate al fin si desta:	is eventually roused to pity:
non fu mai sì gran tempesta,	there was never so great a storm
che non torni il mare in calma.	that the sea failed to return to calm.
Poca stilla un sasso frange,	A few drops of water crack a stone,
non è sempre infelice alma che piange.	a soul which weeps is not unhappy for ever.

Fia diman la sorte amica,	Tomorrow Fortune may be friendly,
s'hoggi è rigida, severa;	though today she is stern and harsh;
doppo lunga aspra fatica,	after long, bitter toil
paga spesso Amor la sera.	love often makes reward in the evening.
Chi non pugna indarno al crine	Whoever does not seize Fortune's locks in vain,
cinger può lauro, o corona.	may surround his head with laurel or a crown.
Solo il premio a quei si dona,	The prize is only given
che del corso giunge al fine.	to the one who reaches the goal.
Non si stanchi, Alma fedele,	Do not tire yourself faithful Soul,
che bel volto non fu sempre crudele.	for a beautiful face was not always cruel.

This sort of text (if often more pessimistic) is commonly set; in this case the music is not complicated, and it could well be considered a triple-time strophic aria. There are two strophes, each of which is divided in two by a prominent central cadence in the tonic. While the choice of metre might seem to lend a less than serious air to the cantata, Carissimi counteracts this by introducing chromatic lines, generally descending, in the continuo part (Ex. 32).

Ex. 32

spe-ri un dì lie - to e con-ten - - - - to

It is hardly an exaggeration to say that no Carissimi cantatas have the same formal structure. *Che dici amore* (S) is also a strophic aria in triple time, but it gains further cohesion through the use of the same words at the beginning and end of each strophe. The famous *Vittoria mio core* (S), which survives in more than a dozen manuscripts, is simply a da capo aria, and owes its popularity to its agreeably tuneful melody. Despite its air of simplicity this cantata is noteworthy for its use of modulation to the dominant before the return of the first section, a possibility not exploited in the other

ABA pieces so far described. In *Sospiri ch'uscite* (S) the *ABA* form is adopted for the music, though the text itself has no repetition; some minor alterations are made to *A* on its second appearance so that certain new words are more effectively underlined; 'acque amare' (bitter waters) has a diminished fifth interval in the melody not present in the first *A*. The pace also slows at the end to suggest a sense of completion.

In other cantatas this da capo form proved susceptible to further development: for instance, *Deh contentatevi* (S) makes more of the contrast between *A* and *B* sections, the latter having a common-time arioso style, as opposed to the triple time of the remainder. In this piece, however, Carissimi briefly recalls the opening music during the central section where the text is the same as that of the opening (Ex. 33). The short reminiscence is less than a tenth of the

Ex. 33

length of the *A* sections, but it none the less hints at a principle of construction much favoured in these cantatas, namely, 'refrain' form.

One of Carissimi's most widely disseminated cantatas, *Bel tempo per me se n'andò* (S), tells how the pursuit of love spells the end of good times and freedom. Though in triple metre throughout, it is punctuated by a refrain which is heard in full three times (*ABABA*). The structure of individual sections is also closely knit: each *B* section comprises two sub-sections, the first of which is in *abb'* form, and the second makes use of transposed repetition of phrases. In *Sempre m'affliggo più* (S), a cantata with an identical formal scheme, the contrasts are heightened, for, while the refrain is in triple metre, the *B* sections adopt a declamatory monodic style (Ex. 34) whose harmonic idiom overshadows even the bold flattened sixths of the refrain. Another cantata in G minor shows that

Ex. 34

Carissimi did not insist on repeating material literally; on its final appearance the refrain to *Io dissi sempre che l'amare* (S) is adapted in two important ways. Some notes are altered so that it fits with the preceding material, and a further phrase is added to secure a more rounded conclusion. Typical of his style is the transposition of a fourth (Ex. 35).

Transformation and adaptation within a given scheme are common features of the cantatas. Though the roots of the genre are close to the strict strophic variation, this is a structural device rarely found in Carissimi's work. *Speranze non partite* (S) is one of the few exceptions: there are three sections, each of which comprises a recitative and aria on the same bass line. The vocal line is different in each section until the words 'andate in pace' are reached; the subsequent passage acts as a type of refrain in the text as well as in the music. That a refrain appears here as a by-product of a different type of musical organization demonstrates how arbitrary any formal categorization of this repertory must be. The same duality is present in *No, no, mio core* (S) where the three strophes each comprise a triple-time aria introduced by an arioso section using related musical material. Here again there is a balance of similar and contrasted material. While the continuo is the same throughout each strophe, only the vocal line of the arioso section is subjected to variation. The concluding aria has the same music for each stanza, and at the end even the text comes into line with the recall of the words of the opening.

The cantata *In un mar di pensieri* (S) also comprises three verses, but there is no introduction and each section contains a triple-metre aria followed by common-time arioso. Each of these six divisions is in *abb'* form, where *b'* is a transposition of *b*. While the self-contained aria section begins and ends in C minor, the arioso, characteristically for the composer, opens in a rather distant tonality (F major) and returns to the tonic by way of a passage of G minor (*b*) followed by its transposition (*b'*). The words of the second half of the arioso function as a refrain—'tocca a me sempre di piangere'—which sums up the sentiment of the whole work. On the second occasion there is an especially expressive response to the text (Ex. 36). Elsewhere in the cantata the vocal line is adapted to

Ex. 36 (Continuo omitted)

toc - ca a   me sem-pre sem-pre   di   pian - - - - -

- - - - ge - re

[it is my lot to cry for ever]

fit the changing text (Ex. 37). Here the continuo line accommodates not only the flat tonality of 'dolor' (sorrows) and the tortuous line of 'fieri' (intense) but also the light embellishment of 'augel' (bird) which takes on a more menacing aspect at 'rapace' (preying). The

Ex. 37

rigid formal organization of many cantatas is tempered by Car' ;simi's attention to detail in responding musically to individual words or sections of text, where he often employs the virtuoso vocal techniques of his day. A single cantata, *Son pur giunta ad amare* (S), provides more than enough material to demonstrate this. It presents the feelings of one who, after many struggles, allowed herself to be trapped by love. Some particularly vivid word-painting is found (Ex. 38).

While the majority of Carissimi's solo cantatas are of the composite type described above, ranging from two to as many as ten contrasting sections, there are a number of arioso pieces which, like the simple arias, maintain that style throughout. *E pur volete piangere* (S), another Benigni setting, comprises three sections linked by common concluding phrases and central exclamations of 'Lasso' (all a result of the poetic text). Sustained notes in the continuo part provide the basis for a declamatory vocal line; the dissonance in the initial bar is a hallmark of Carissimi's monodic

Ex. 38 (Continuo omitted)

writing (Ex. 39). Some cantatas in which the arioso style predominates admit short aria passages for contrast without their fulfilling any structural role. The largely arioso *Risvegliatemi pensieri* (S) includes a short central triple-metre passage punctuated twice by a continuo *ritornello*, and also breaks into that metre in order to emphasize the two lines which constitute the crux of the poet's feelings:

In sonno placide le luci languide già s'addormentano,
Fantasmi horribili con fieri imagini già mi spaventano.

In sleep the gentle languid eyes are already resting,
Horrible ghosts with their fierce shapes are already frightening me.

Two arias, one in quadruple, the other in triple time, are
introduced in the course of *Insuperbito il Tebro* (S), another basically
declamatory work. These interjections, the first through-composed,
and the second comprising three strophes, do not invest the work
with the same complexity of internal relationships in a cantata such
as *In un mar di pensieri*. Fresh material is constantly presented, even
though there are some deliberate efforts to secure cohesion—for
instance, the insertion of the short continuo *ritornello* leading the
first aria into the recitative.

An equal spectrum of diversity is presented in the ensemble
cantatas which represent about a quarter of Carissimi's output. In
these the tradition of the amorous pastoral dialogue is carried
forward. The most widely circulated cantata in this repertory is
Sciolto havean dall'alte sponde, on which Carissimi composed a
parody mass. The cantata survives in thirteen manuscripts, while its
final trio is preserved in an additional sixteen sources. If any work
can be considered the secular counterpart of the oratorio, it is this.
Subtitled *I Naviganti*, it tells of two lovers (SS) on the troubled sea
of love who are urged to return to land by the third voice (a
baritone) as the storm gathers. The tutti has the task of setting the
scene and supplying a final comment, while the two lovers lament
individually and together. Unified by its strict adherence to a C
minor tonality, further cohesion is gained through considerable
economy of material. While the work is framed by prolonged
triple-metre trio sections, there is also a certain amount of
repeated material:

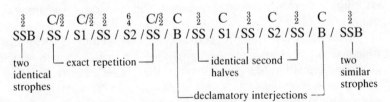

In addition a five-bar continuo *ritornello* is heard after each strophe
of the opening trio, and follows all but one of the duets.

Despite the work's fine construction, the tableau-like approach
of *I Naviganti* does militate against the more natural dialogue style
which is found elsewhere in the repertory. In *Per mille colpi* (SS)

there is an almost operatic alternation of voices in a style approaching simple recitative. This piece shows the extent to which the genre could be a successful vehicle for representation: the characters, Pietà and Amore, sympathize with a blind beggar—not represented musically—who has entered the pastoral landscape. Generally the subject matter is more orthodox, and three of the ensemble cantatas are dialogues between the stock pastoral characters of Tirsi and Filli. One of these is among Carissimi's earliest published works, *Io corro alle sventure* (SS) of 1646. The characters first sing lengthy solo passages: Tirsi accuses Filli of being unfaithful and Filli responds by pledging her fidelity. Having resolved the issue, the voices unite in a simple duet which alternates between straightforward, not too prolonged counterpoint, and flowing parallel sixths and thirds in which the pair reaffirm their mutual affection. Despite the simplicity of the overall form, further structural devices are introduced in the two solo passages: each of these is punctuated by an identical aria lasting eight semibreves in common time.

One third of the ensemble duets are strophic settings, and in *Io corro alle sventure* Carissimi uses this form for the final duet, incorporating it into a larger form. The independent strophic duets adopt the two-voiced texture for musical rather than dramatic reasons, and there is little sense of characterization. Carissimi is none the less careful to set in this way texts in which there is a reasonable degree of correspondence between the verses. For instance, in *Fuggi quel ben* the word 'fuggi' (flee) is replaced by 'corre' (run), and 'lusinga' (flatter) by 'piagenti' (crying) in the second strophe. Such strophic settings must have been widely performed, and manuscript evidence would suggest that the strophic ensemble cantata replaced the madrigal in amateur musical activity.

These relatively simple settings are far removed from the polished musical style of *Le ferite d'un cor* (SST), a trio which achieved considerable popularity at the French court in 1656. There are no characters as such in this cantata, but the conventional theme of unrequited love is expounded in a series of arias and recitatives for two sopranos and tenor with opening and concluding trios. Sometimes a concern for unity in the cantatas caused Carissimi to repeat the opening trio by way of conclusion, as in *E chi vi resta più* (SS) and *Il mio cor è un mar di pianti* (SS), which are both in four main sections.

Despite this preoccupation with formal cohesion, Carissimi only rarely follows the previous generation in using stock bass figurations such as dominated the Roman secular cantata at the hands of composers like Cifra. Only in *Tra più riposti abissi* (SSB, 2 vlns) is there any suggestion of the descending tetrachord achieving some importance throughout a cantata. Though it appears at least once in most sections, and with considerable prominence in the *ritornelli* for two violins, it by no means performs the role of an ostinato.

Refrain form occurs here as well as in the solo cantatas. One example of this structure occurs in a trio cantata, *A piè d'un verde alloro*; the refrain, the section with major-minor alternation for setting the words 'laughing' and 'crying', was made famous through the critical attention it received from both Kircher and Charles Burney. This type of tonal shift is not unique in Carissimi's output: the two voice cantata *Ahi, non torna* uses a similar device in the same tonality of F. The cantata, *A piè d'un verde alloro* is perhaps of more interest because of its protagonists who are not the usual lovers, but rather philosophers, Heraclitus and Democritus. Disappointment in love (yet again) is the substance of their discourse; they are of contrasting dispositions, one melancholy and the other more phlegmatic in their attitude towards thwarted love. This difference is underlined by the musical setting, and the text is particularly well ordered in the way it alternates lines for both voices with solo phrases.

While this cantata can be regarded as faintly amusing—a rare quality in this repertory—there is one work which is genuinely humorous: *Poiché lo Sdegno intese ch'amor* (SSS), also called *Il Ciarlatano*. For once a cantata suggests a cure other than death for the pains of love: the central character, the Charlatan, claims to have an alternative remedy, which he puts into practice through deriding the whole idea of passion. After an introduction, in which he is announced and his skills outlined, the Charlatan tries to hawk his wares and, in a series of recitatives, boasts of his previous successes. These are only interrupted by a trio sung by his followers in support of his claims and a bipartite duet lamenting the fact that lovers are so credulous. The cantata ends with the trio of 'compagni' proclaiming how the cure has been effective for them and praising its inventor. The recitative is *parlando* throughout, and has little in common with the flowing ariosos which dominate most of the other cantatas. This arises from the need to

Ex. 40

set a lengthy, factual text in a dispassionate manner (Ex. 40).

Only the libretto of the pastoral *L'amorose passioni di Fileno* survives as evidence that Carissimi tried his hand at dramatic writing on a larger scale. It was published in Bologna in 1647 and performed there at a meeting of the *accademia* which met in the house of one Signor Casali. No connection has been established between Carissimi and Bologna, so it would be reasonable to assume that it was originally intended for a Roman academy. Solo singers represent the poet, Fileno, and Love, and choruses personify Hope, Fear, and Thought. The plot is typical of pastoral drama both in its setting and its use of allegory:

The shepherd Fileno, lover of Nerea, having attended her thanklessly for a long time, is close to desperation and is comforted by Hope and then assaulted by Fear. Experiencing the two emotions of hope and fear at the same time he requests help from Counsel and for this is reproved by Love. At this he resolves to follow his beloved faithfully. Finally, while he sleeps, Desires appear in a dance, following the vision of the beloved.

The anonymous poetic text of this pastoral has much in common with those of the cantatas, and one can surmise that it was set using a similar combination of arioso and aria.

VI
CONCLUSION

THE greatest problem in making an assessment of Carissimi is our continuing lack of information about his contemporaries. Little work has yet been undertaken on those figures who were active in Rome during the period of Carissimi's maturity. Only with Stradella does the situation improve.[1] While there is no disputing Carissimi's outstanding importance, he was only one of the many composers who provided music for the churches and courts of the city. Luigi Rossi was arguably his most distinguished Roman contemporary, but it would be wrong to regard him as a rival since their careers took very different paths.[2] Although Rossi held the post of organist (with occasional absences) at San Luigi dei Francesi for twenty years until his death in 1653, he was mainly active in noble Roman households. He served two papal families— the Borghese and the Barberini—and, following his operatic success in Rome, spent much of the last decade of his life in Paris at the invitation of Mazarin. His *œuvre* reflects this difference in emphasis; while there remains only a handful of motets and vernacular oratorios, about three hundred cantatas can be identified as his. Between his cantatas and those of Carissimi, one notices considerable formal differences. Rossi favoured the short, homogenous aria with a flowing, song-like vocal line, perhaps punctuated by a brief contrasting section; straightforward binary and refrain forms abound. Only about one fifth of his cantatas are divided into sections of contrasting character. In most of Carissimi's cantatas the sections are more extended than in Rossi's, and show greater variety; formally they are considerably more complex, making less use of strophic organization. Rossi was clearly considered to be the foremost cantata composer around 1640, since Pietro Della Valle cited his *Hor che la notte* as an example of the serious cantata in his informative treatise *Della musica dell'età nostra* (1640).[3] As we have seen, Carissimi appears to have come to the genre later and to have developed its more formally complex aspects. Carissimi's penchant for contrast and sectionalization may well be related to his treatment of dramatic situations in the oratorios.

It was in the field of opera that Rossi eventually won most recognition: the success of his *Il palazzo incantato* in 1642 led to the composition of *Orfeo* in Paris some five years later. Rossi's initial operatic venture was the outcome of Cardinal Antonio Barberini's discerning patronage; the Barberini were clearly the only Roman family in a position to commission such a work. Until his involvement with the more modest court of Christine of Sweden, Carissimi's musical activities largely revolved around those of the religious establishments where he was employed. His *L'amorose passioni di Fileno* is more an extension of the pastoral cantata than a fully developed operatic work.

A large proportion of Carissimi's output was intended for church use, and in this field Rossi ceases to be the best point of comparison. As the organist at San Luigi for many years, Rossi seems to have left church composition to the succession of distinguished maestri; or else the bulk of the works he wrote have been lost. Other composers' music furnishes closer parallels to Carissimi as far as sacred music is concerned. Whereas Carissimi appears to have been active in the formal development of the cantata, he was prepared to take the motet as he found it. The composition of motets as a number of short, contrasting sections had already become common by the time Carissimi arrived in Rome. Only on musical grounds, and because of certain distinctive turns of phrase, can one try to distinguish the work of Carissimi from that of his contemporaries in this field. There were other composers of distinction in Rome at the time and these deserve to be better known; after 1650 the names of Francesco Foggia and Bonifazio Graziani are the most noteworthy. The similarities between their works and those of Carissimi are much greater than any differences that might be noted.

As regards the oratorio, a genre explored by relatively few composers, Domenico Mazzocchi emerges alongside Carissimi as the other figure of stature. The works of both composers follow the same formal patterns, but Mazzocchi is often more angular, and even wayward, both in his melodic lines and in his approach to counterpoint.[4] His music is none the worse for lacking the poised symmetry which characterizes much of Carissimi's writing.

If Carissimi was no isolated figure at home, it should not be forgotten that his was the name most frequently heard abroad. A number of factors contributed to his widespread fame. Perhaps most important was his contact with an unending stream of singers (both Italian and German) who passed through the German College and went on to distinguish themselves in Northern Europe.[5] One example of a singer who followed this path was Kaspar Förster; born in Gdańsk in 1616, he studied with Carissimi in the mid-1630s and subsequently took up posts in Warsaw, Venice, and Copenhagen, as well as his native city. Another musician, the Roman Vincenzo Alberici, was at the German College between 1641 and 1646, and his career later took him to the musical centres of Dresden, Stockholm, Hamburg, London, Berlin, Leipzig, and Prague.

The vogue for Italian culture at the French court from the 1640s meant that a number of singers from the German College were invited to Paris to take part in performances of works by Rossi, Cavalli, and Lully. It may well have been this influx which prompted Charpentier to study with Carissimi in Rome. After all, Carissimi's music was known at the French court from at least 1656. It is not difficult to discern Carissimi's influence in Charpentier's works; take, for instance, the latter's *Pestis mediolanensis* with its simple opening prelude, its fundamentally Italianate arioso, and the bold, declamatory double-choir writing. Clearly Charpentier assimilated many of his master's mannerisms, including the use of particular harmonic devices to highlight the text. Charpentier's pattern of employment enabled him to explore many of the genres with which Carissimi was also particularly involved. Here one finds certain similarities: Charpentier's Jesuit connections made him the only composer besides Carissimi to contribute in a substantial way to the Latin oratorio. His large number of small-scale motets also betrays the Italian influence, and research into Charpentier's secular, dramatic music could well cast some light on our understanding of Carissimi's output. Pitoni remarked that Carissimi was active 'not only in church compositions, but also in chamber works and theatre, as in his *commedie* preserved in the [German] College'.[6] Unfortunately that is about all the information we have concerning Carissimi's dramatic music.

In England, too, Carissimi began to build up a reputation in the 1660s. Diarists such as Mortoft mention him in their writings, while Charles II's interest in Italian music meant that he kept a number of Italian musicians at court, among them Alberici. Pepys, writing in London in 1664, told of an evening spent 'singing the best piece of musique, counted of all hands in the world, made by Seignor Charissimi the famous master in Rome'. Some indication of Carissimi's popularity can be gained from numerous musical sources of his work which survive in English manuscripts. While Purcell copied music by Cazzati and Monteverdi, other figures were responsible for the Carissimi manuscripts which have survived. George Jeffreys, the composer, copied some of the earliest English manuscripts of Carissimi's works. Far more important was the contribution of Henry Aldrich, Dean of Christ Church, Oxford. His extensive transcriptions contain a good deal of music by Carissimi, and Aldrich's attraction to Carissimi's style is witnessed in the number of his anthems which derive their melodic material from works by Carissimi. Another substantial corpus of manuscripts comes from the collection of Richard Goodson the Elder, who was also associated with Christ Church and held the post of Professor of Music in Oxford from 1682 until his death in 1718. It is impossible to say whether Handel encountered Carissimi's works during his time in Rome or on arrival in England. He was in any case impressed by what he knew, since he inserted a section of recitative from *Jephte* into *Alexander's Feast*; moreover, he took the final chorus of *Jephte* and transformed it into the distinctly un-Handelian chorus, 'Hear, Jacob's God', in *Samson*.

Carissimi's influence had spread widely throughout Europe even during his lifetime. Although his memory has lived on through his oratorios, a fuller appreciation of his stature is felt with the realization that he was important for both the development of the cantata *and* motet. Athanasius Kircher, a contemporary Jesuit writer, expressed this opinion of Carissimi in his *Musurgia universalis*:

The most excellent Iacomo Carissimi, a composer of great fame, most worthy *maestro di cappella* of the Church of S Apollinare of the German College for a period of many years, outshines others in originality and in ease of compositional style, moving the spirits of the listeners into many moods; for his compositions are full of life and a vivacity of spirit . . .[7]

It is worth remembering that in 1650, when those words were written, Carissimi was less than halfway through his Roman career.

NOTES

CHAPTER I

[1] On Carissimi's time at the German College see T. D. Culley, *A Study of the Musicians connected with the German College in Rome during the 17th Century and of their Activities in Northern Europe*, Jesuits and Music, i (Rome, 1970), pp. 171–274.

[2] Culley, op. cit., pp. 166–7.

[3] O. Panciroli, *I tesori nascosti nell'alma città di Roma* (Rome, 1600), p. 224: 'It is not necessary to mention the refinement and sweetness with which the divine office is celebrated because everyone is aware of this.'

[4] On the musical establishment at Tivoli see G. Radiciotti, *L'arte musicale in Tivoli nei secoli XVI, XVII e XVIII* (Tivoli, 1921).

[5] Culley, op. cit., p. 134.

CHAPTER II

[1] The seminal article in this area is G. Massenkeil, 'Die Wiederholungs-figuren in den Oratorien Giacomo Carissimis', *Archiv für Musikwissen-schaft*, xiii (1956), 42–60.

[2] The instructive preface to his *Cento concerti ecclesiastici* (Venice, 1602) is printed in English translation in O. Strunk, *Source Readings in Music History* (London, 1950), 419–23.

[3] *Motecta singulis, binis, ternisque vocibus concinenda, una cum basso ad organum accomodata* (Rome, 1609; repr. Rome, 1620).

[4] From *Dialogici concentus, senis, octonisque vocibus . . . nunc primum in lucem edite, opus decimumsextum* (Venice, 1613).

[5] From *RISM* 1645².

[6] F. Mortoft, *His Book being His Travels through France and Italy*, ed. M. Letts (London, 1925), p. 163 (21 March, 1659).

[7] More subjective texts occur, however, in the group of motets intended for use at Eucharistic devotions or for spiritual recreation.

[8] From *Sacrae modulationes . . . pars tertia, una cum basso ad organum* (Rome 1628).

[9] In *Psalmi vespertini quatuor integris vocibus in organo concinendi . . . liber II, opus tertium* (Rome, 1642).

[10] On these works see H. W. Hitchcock, 'The Latin Oratorios of Marc-Antoine Charpentier', *Musical Quarterly*, xli (1955), 41–65.

[11] In *Lapidabunt Stephanum a 2* from *Liber secundus diversarum modulationum binis, ternis, quaternis ac quinis vocibus* (Rome, 1616)

[12] From *RISM* 1618[3].

[13] A. Kircher, *Musurgia universalis* (2 vols., Rome, 1650), i, p. 603.

[14] Kircher, op. cit., i, p. 598.

CHAPTER III

[1] It is known that he was offered the post of maestro at St Mark's, Venice on the death of Monteverdi (1643), and Archduke Leopold William, son of the Holy Roman Emperor Ferdinand II, tried unsuccessfully to secure his services in 1647. A letter survives in which Carissimi declines the post of maestro at an unspecified cathedral (see A. V. Jones, *The Motets of Carissimi* (2 vols., Ann Arbor, 1982), i, pp. 9–11).

[2] G. Massenkeil, 'Über die Messen Giacomo Carissimis', *Analecta musicologica*, i (1963), 28–37.

[3] This survives in *GB-Lbl*, Add. MS 5054.

[4] W. Witzenmann, 'Una messa no di Carissimi, un'altra sì', *Studi musicali*, xi (1982), 61–89.

[5] Prolonged *ostinati* went out of fashion in Rome in the late 1620s, even in secular music. This suggests that the mass could be an early work of Carissimi; after all, the counterpoint of the two early *Regina caeli* settings in the Assisi manuscript is hardly polished.

[6] These survive in *I-Bc*, MSS Z.143 and Z.84.

[7] Culley, *A Study of the Musicians*, pp. 198–9.

[8] *Davidis Cithara Psalmorum quatuor vocum concentibus concors . . . cum*

basso ad organum (Rome, 1615) and *Octo Magnificat, in singulis tonis, quaternis vocibus concinendis . . . opus quartum* (Rome, 1616).

⁹ *I-Bc*, MS Q.43.

CHAPTER IV

¹ On the general history of the Congregazione dell'Oratorio see H. E. Smither, *The Oratorio in the Baroque Era: Italy, Vienna, Paris* (Chapel Hill, 1977), pp. 39–76. An account of the context for the performance of the Latin oratorio is given in G. Dixon, 'Oratorio o mottetto? Alcune reflessioni sulla classificazione della musica sacra del Seicento', *Nuova rivista musicale italiana*, vii (1983), 203–22.

² Quoted in D. Alaleona, *Studi su la storia dell'oratorio musicale in Italia* (Turin, 1908), p. 262.

³ Smither, op. cit., p. 219.

⁴ This work is called *Vanitas vanitatum II* in the IISM edition. *Vanitas vanitatum I* cannot seriously be considered as Carissimi's work on stylistic grounds.

⁵ In *Motetti, e dialoghi a otto voci, concertati con voci sole, con doi bassi seguiti per il primo, & secondo organo . . . libro secondo* (Rome, 1627).

⁶ In *Sacrae modulationes . . . pars secunda, una cum basso ad organum* (Venice, 1628).

⁷ *Psalmi vespertini binis choris concinendi* (Rome, 1648); examples from two of these works are found in G. Dixon, 'Liturgical Music in Rome (1605–45)' (2 vols, Ph.D. diss., University of Durham, 1982), ii, pp. 278–82.

⁸ Mortoft, *His Book*, pp. 145 and 163.

⁹ Smither, op. cit., p. 237.

¹⁰ Printed in A. Liess, 'Materialen zur römischen Musikgeschichte des Seicento: Musikerlisten des Oratorio San Marcello 1664–1725', *Acta musicologica*, xxix (1957), 137–71.

¹¹ Rome, Archivio del Vicariato, Archives of the Arciconfraternita dell' Orazione e Morte, Libro 208, *Libro del Camerieno 1618.1619.16xx.16xxi*, fol. 82.

¹² Mortoft, *His Book*, p. 146.

[13] L. Bianchi in the preface to his edition of the *Oratorio della SS Vergine*, p. xiii.

[14] Smither, op. cit., pp. 182–4.

CHAPTER V

[1] *Cantade et arie* (Venice, 1620); this is the second edition of a work presumably printed a few years earlier.

[2] On his appointment to the court of Christine of Sweden see Culley, *A Study of the Musicians*, pp. 178–9.

[3] Mortoft, *His Book*, p. 97 (7 January, 1659).

CHAPTER VI

[1] C. Gianturco, *The Life and Works of Alessandro Stradella* (Oxford, forthcoming).

[2] A. Ghizlanzoni, *Luigi Rossi: biografia e analisi delle composizioni* (Milan, 1954).

[3] Edited in A. Solerti, *Le origini del melodramma: testimonianze dei contemporanei* (Turin, 1903, repr. Bologna, 1969), pp. 148–79, esp. p. 168.

[4] Cf. D. Mazzocchi, *Sacrae concertationes* ed. W. Witzenmann (Cologne, 1975).

[5] T. D. Culley, 'The Influence of the German College in Rome on Music in German Speaking Countries during the Sixteenth and Seventeenth Centuries', *Analecta musicologica*, vii (1969), 1–35; ix (1970), 20–63.

[6] Pitoni's notes on Carissimi are found in Cappella Giulia MS I, 2 (2), *Notizia de'contrapuntisti e compositori di musica . . .*, pp. 683–4.

[7] A. Kircher, *Musurgia universalis* (2 vols., Rome, 1650), i, p. 603.

WORKS IN MODERN EDITIONS

No complete list of Carissimi's works is included here as an adequate catalogue is already available in *New Grove*. Detailed catalogues relating to specific genres have also been compiled by A. V. Jones for the motets, and Gloria Rose for the cantatas. I. M. Buff, *A Thematic Catalog of the Sacred Works of Giacomo Carissimi* (Clifton, New Jersey, 1979) is a misleading volume since the author has been uncritical in assessing attributions; some pieces listed as authentic are simply not admissible on stylistic grounds.

ABBREVIATIONS

IISM: G. Carissimi, *Le opere complete*, ed. L. Bianchi and others, Istituto italiano per la storia della musica, Monumenti, III (Rome, 1951–)
Jeppesen: K. Jeppesen, *La Flora* (3 vols., Copenhagen, 1949)
Jones: A. V. Jones, *The Motets of Carissimi* (2 vols., Ann Arbor, 1982)
Rose: G. Carissimi, *Six Solo Cantatas*, ed. G. Rose (London, 1969)

MASSES

Missa a 3 voci (TTB/SSB) [doubtful, see p. 17], IISM, *Messe e motetti*, i, 1
Missa septimi toni (SATB, SATB) [doubtful] in L. Torchi, ed., *L'arte musicale in Italia* (7 vols., Milan, 1897–1908), v, 1

PSALMS

Confitebor tibi Domine (SSB) in Jones, ii, 281
Dixit Dominus (SSATB) ed. J. Pilgrim (Hilversum, 1968)

MOTETS

Alma redemptoris (SSB) in Jones, ii, 221
Anima nostra sustinet (SS) in Jones, ii, 229
Annunciate gentes (SSATB) in Jones, ii, 236; ed. N. M. Jensen (Egtved, 1967)
Ardens est cor nostrum (SATB) in Jones, ii, 250

Audite sancti (SSB/ATB) in Jones, ii, 260
Benedictus Deus et Pater (SSS) in Jones, ii, 269
Cantabo Domino (SS) in Jones, ii, 274
Christus factus est (SSATB, SATB) ed. L. Feininger, Documenta liturgiae
   polychoralis, xviii (Rome, 1964)
Cum reverteretur (SSS) in IISM, *Messe e motetti*, i, 74
Desiderata nobis (ATB) in Jones, ii, 299
Dicite nobis (SSAT) in Jones, ii, 308
Domine Deus meus (S/B) in Jones, ii, 319; ed. R. Ewerhart, Cantio sacra,
   viii (Cologne, 1956)
Domine quis habitabit (SST) in Jones, ii, 327
Duo ex discipulis Jesu (SST) in IISM, *Oratori*, vi, 12
Emendemus in melius (SAT) in Jones, ii, 338
Exulta gaude filia Sion (SS) in Jones, ii, 345
Exurge cor meum (S, 2 vlns) in Jones, ii, 354
Hodie Simon Petrus ascendit (TT) in IISM, *Messe e motetti*, i, 68
Hymnum jucunditatis cantemus (SS) in Jones, ii, 364
Insurrexerunt in nos (SAT) in Jones, ii, 372
Jubilemus omnes et cantemus (SSB) ed. Ebbe Selen (Uppsala, 1972)
Laudemus virum gloriosum (SS) in Jones, ii, 382
Militia est vita hominis (SSB) in Jones, ii, 389
Mortalis homo (S) in Jones, ii, 407
O dulcissimum Mariae nomen (SS) in Jones, ii, 413
O ignis sancte (SS) in Jones, ii, 417
O quam pulchra es (S) in Jones, ii, 424
O vulnera doloris (B) ed. R. Ewerhart, Cantio sacra, xvi (Cologne, 1958)
Parce heu, parce jam (SATB) ed. J. Pilgrim (Hilversum, 1971)
Plaudite caelestes chori (S) in Jones, ii, 433
Quis est hic vir (SSS) in Jones, ii, 438
Quomodo facti sunt impii (SSB) in Jones, ii, 449
Salve puellule (S) ed. R. Ewerhart, Cantio sacra, xlviii (Cologne, 1961)
Salve regina (SSB) in Jones, ii, 455
Si qua est consolatio (SSB) in Jones, ii, 464
Sicut stella matutina (S) in Jones, ii, 472
Suscitavit Dominus (ATB) in Jones, ii, 482
Timete Dominum (SSATB) in Jones, ii, 495
Viderunt te Domine (SB) in Jones, ii, 517

ORATORIOS

LATIN
Historia di Abraham et Isaac (SATTB) in IISM, *Oratori*, ii, 1
Baltazar (SSATB), IISM, *Oratori*, iii; ed. F. Chrysander, Denkmäler der
   Tonkunst, ii (Bergedorf, 1869), 50

Damnatorum lamentatio (ATB) in Jones, ii, 504; ed. C. dell'Argine
  (Florence, 1972)
Historia divitis (SATB, SATB), IISM, *Oratori*, v
Ezechia (SSATB, 2 vlns) in IISM, *Oratori*, i, 14
Felicitas beatorum (SSS) ed. C. dell'Argine (Florence, 1972)
Jephte (SSSATB) ed. F. Chrysander, Denkmäler der Tonkunst, ii
  (Bergedorf, 1869), 2; also by J. E. Beat (London, 1974)
Job (SAB) in IISM, *Oratori*, i, 1
Jonas (SATB, SSATB) ed. F. Chrysander, Denkmäler der Tonkunst, ii
  (Bergedorf, 1869), 84
Judicium extremum (SSATB, ATB, ATB), IISM, *Oratori*, iv
Judicium Salomonis (SSAB) ed. F. Chrysander, Denkmäler der Tonkunst,
  ii, (Bergedorf, 1869), 30
Vanitas Vanitatum (SSATB) in IISM, *Oratori*, X, 8

ITALIAN
Daniele (SSSATB), IISM, *Oratori*, vii
Oratorio della SS Vergine (SSATB), IISM, *Oratori*, viii

CANTATAS

Ahi non torna (SS) in IISM, *Cantate*, i, 12
Amor mio, che cosa è questa (S) in Rose, 30
Apritevi inferni (S) in Rose, 54
Bel tempo per me (S) in Rose, 19
Cara e dolce mia vita (S) in IISM, *Cantate*, ii, 15
Che legge è questa (S) in IISM, *Cantate*, ii, 29
Come sete importuni (S) in Jeppesen, i, 31
Deh memoria e che più chiedi (S) in Rose, 37
Dunque degl'horti miei (S) in IISM, *Cantate*, i, 1
In un mar di pensieri (S) in Rose, 44
La mia fede altrui giurata (S) ed. L. Landshoff, *Alte Meister des Bel Canto*
  (Leipzig, 1912–27), i, 57
Lungi da me fuggite (S) in Jeppesen, i, 26
Non chiede altro che vita (S) in R. Haas, *Die Musik des Barocks*, (Potsdam,
  1928), 127
No, no, non si speri (A) ed. L. Landshoff, *Alte Meister des Bel Canto*, i, 49
Non posso vivere (S) in Jeppesen, i, 38
O se mai di quell'arsura (SS) in IISM, *Cantate*, ii, 59
Peregrin d'ignote sponde (SS) in IISM, *Cantate*, ii, 59
Poiché lo sdegno intese (SSS) in L. Torchi, ed., *L'arte musicale in Italia*, v,
  238
Rimanti in pace homai (ST) in Jeppesen, iii, 99
Sciolto havean dall'alte sponde (SSBar) in IISM, *Cantate*, i, 20
Scrivete, occhi dolenti (S) in IISM, *Cantate*, ii, 43
Soccorretemi, ch'io moro (S) ed. L. Landshoff, *Alte Meister des Bel Canto*, i, 40

Socorretemi per pietà (SS) in Jeppesen, iii, 101
Suonerà l'ultima tromba (S) in Rose, 68
Sventura, cor mio (S) in Jeppesen, ii, 28
Vittoria, mio core (S) in Jeppesen, i, 23

SELECT BIBLIOGRAPHY

A. Cametti, 'Primo contributo per una biografia di Giacomo Carissimi', *Rivista musicale italiana*, xxiv (1917), 379–417

T. D. Culley, *A Study of the Musicians connected with the German College in Rome during the 17th century and of their Activities in Northern Europe*, Jesuits and Music, i (Rome, 1970)

G. Dixon, 'Liturgical Music in Rome (1605–45)' (Ph.D. diss., University of Durham, 1982)

——, 'Lenten Devotions: some *memoriae* of Baroque Rome', *Musical Times*, cxxiv (1983), 157–61

——, 'Oratorio o mottetto? Alcune reflessioni sulla classificazione della musica sacra del Seicento', *Nuova rivista musicale italiana*, vii (1983), 203–22

N. C. Fortune, 'Italian Secular Monody from 1600 to 1635: an Introductory Survey', *Musical Quarterly*, xxxiv (1953), 171–95

A. V. Jones, *The Motets of Carissimi* (2 vols., Ann Arbor, 1982)

G. Massenkeil, 'Die Wiederholungsfiguren in den Oratorien Giacomo Carissimis', *Archiv für Musikwissenschaft*, xiii (1956), 42–60

——, 'Über die Messen Giacomo Carissimis', *Analecta musicologica*, i (1963), 28–37

G. Rose, 'The Cantatas of Giacomo Carissimi', *Musical Quarterly*, xlviii (1962), 204–15

——, *Giacomo Carissimi*, Wellesley Edition Cantata Index Series, no. 5 (Wellesley College, 1966)

C. Sartori and G. M. Manusardi, *Giacomo Carissimi: catalogo delle opere attribuite* (Milan, 1975)

H. E. Smither, 'The Latin Dramatic Dialogue and the Nascent Oratorio', *Journal of the American Musicological Society*, xx (1967), 403–33

——, 'Carissimi's Latin Oratorios: their Terminology, Functions and Position in Oratorio History', *Analecta musicologica*, xi (1976), 54–78

——, *A History of the Oratorio*, i: *The Oratorio in the Baroque Era: Italy, Vienna, Paris* (Chapel Hill, 1977)

W. Witzenmann, 'Una messa no di Carissimi, un'altra sì', *Studi musicali*, xi (1982), 61–89

INDEX OF WORKS

The purpose of the series *Oxford Studies of Composers* is to provide short, scholarly, critical surveys of composers about whom no major work is already available, or whose music is in need of re-assessment. The emphasis is on the music itself, biographical data being kept to a minimum.

Carissimi (1605–74) was a crucial figure in the development of the baroque oratorio, cantata, and *concertato* motet. In his day, Carissimi's reputation was as great as that of Monteverdi, and his music directly influenced works by many composers, including Charpentier and Handel. This book is the first in any language to offer a critical survey of Carissimi's music and to place him into the mainstream of baroque musical life in Rome.

Other books in this series

ISBN 0-19-315243-6

OXFORD UNIVERSITY PRESS

77974
111